Also by Clare Gibson

The Secret Life of Dreams

The Dreamer's Almanac

How to Read Symbols

Signs and Symbols:
A Guide to their Meaning and Origins

The Hidden Life of the Ancient Maya

The Hidden Life of Ancient Egypt

The Hidden Life of Art

The Hidden Life of Renaissance Art

Sacred Symbols

Symbols of the Goddess

IN THE MOMENT

Interpreting Dreams

Clare Gibson

Saraband

Published by Saraband
3 Clairmont Gardens
Glasgow, G3 7LW
www.saraband.net

*The interpretations in this book are based on those in a
previous work by Clare Gibson with M. Jane Taylor.*

ISBN: 9781913393939
eISBN: 9781915089977

Printed and bound in Great Britain by Clays Ltd,
Elcograf S.p.A.

1 2 3 4 5 6 7 8 9 1

MIX
Paper | Supporting
responsible forestry
FSC® C018072

"Dreams—a microscope through which we look at the hidden occurrences in our soul."

Erich Fromm

Contents

Introduction

Why do we dream? And what do our dreams mean? These questions have always intrigued us. Although many theories have been proposed, no one knows for sure, not least because our dreams are so personal. That said, certain common factors can certainly influence what we dream about, as well as how our sleeping selves react to the visions and sounds playing out in our minds.

As individuals, our personal experiences and memories – good and bad – hopes and fears, friends and foes all play a part in our dreams. More generally, events in the wider world can affect our dreams, too, especially in recent years, when we have endured chaos, turbulence and uncertainty precipitated by a deadly pandemic, escalating climate change, war in Europe, dramatic political events, terrorism and religious extremism, social intolerance, polarizing culture wars, increasing financial worries and more besides. We have very little control over these unsettling global events and trends, or over their effects on us, which contributes to our anxiety. When this fearfulness surfaces in our dreams, recognizing such stressors, and perhaps taking small, practical steps in response that help you to feel more in control, even if it's only avoiding news bulletins, may have positive results, be it in real life or in the dream world.

Headline news apart, other things that we see online can influence our dreams, especially if we are constantly monitoring social media. This can be especially pernicious at bedtime, when an over-stimulated brain, flooded by a fast-moving stream of images and messages – sometimes aggressive, violent or upsetting – can result in insomnia or night after night of fitful sleep punctuated by troubled dreams. If this rings true for you, stopping the constant bombardment by switching off electronic devices well before bedtime and letting your mind relax and unwind may work wonders in improving the quality of your sleep and your enjoyment of your dreams.

People tend to remember troubling dreams far more than pleasant ones, especially nightmares and recurring dreams – and, indeed, recurring night-mares. Some such dreams reflect an issue that you already know is bothering you, perhaps a looming exam, a dental appointment or a social ordeal that you are dreading. Less straightforward to understand are dreams that seem to make no sense, but that, on waking, stay with you and leave you feeling somehow unsettled. These may be your unconscious mind's expression of fears or anxieties that you may have repressed rather than face up to, in which case they may be sending you a message that addressing your fear, examining the root of your anxiety and trying to resolve it, or at least come to terms with it, could result in more tranquil nights. Even just identifying a negative issue and acknowledging its existence may help to put your unconscious mind to rest. Similarly, traumatic experiences may be relived or replayed in dreams, reflecting the psychological damage that has been done. Again, it may be that taking the time in the light of day calmly and rationally to think the dream through will help you to understand what may have triggered it, and then to consider how best to respond in the waking world.

The unconscious mind does not always express itself clearly, so pondering the possibility that an aspect of your dream symbolized something else may give you the key to interpreting it. Could a dream of falling have represented a fear of failing, for instance? Or did you have a metaphorical dream, in which, perhaps, desperately floundering in water signified feeling out of your depth? Could a dream of hurtling headlong down a slope have expressed a feeling of going downhill fast? The various types of dreams and interpretative tips discussed in this book provide an insight into how your unconscious mind works, giving you the tools with which to tease out a dream's meaning.

Not all dreams mean doom and gloom, however. Some can be so unthreateningly bizarre that you wake up feeling amused and bemused. They may be fun for your waking mind to revisit, but if, on reflection, you cannot find any meaning in a dream like this, you can at least salute your unconscious mind's inventive imagination.

Whatever your motivation, taking the time to think about and analyse your dreams can be rewarding. Not only can interpreting your dreams give you a better understanding of your psyche and highlight aspects of your life and relationships of which you might otherwise have been unaware, but it may also result in sweeter dreams and a sounder night's sleep.

Sleep hath its own world,
And a wide realm of wild reality,
And dreams in their development have breath,
And tears, and tortures, and the touch of joy;
They have a weight upon our waking thoughts,
They take a weight from off our waking toils,
They do divide our being.

Lord Byron, 'The Dream' (1816)

Part 1:
What Are Dreams?

About Our Dreams

Dreams have always intrigued and puzzled people. We know this from the lore that we have inherited from ancient civilizations the world over, from the tales of mysterious and powerful dreams that were initially handed down from generation to generation by word of mouth before eventually being recorded in more permanent form by means of writing and drawings. The Aborigines of Australia, for example, tell of the Dreamtime, or Dreaming, the primeval period when their ancestors brought the landscape and every creature—humankind included—that inhabits it into being, and continue to celebrate this magical, mythical era in their artistic traditions and sacred rites.

A Brief History of Dreams

The first dreams to have been set down in writing are thought to have been those contained in the *Epic of Gilgamesh,* a stirring piece of ancient Babylonian literature that is believed to date from around 1760 B.C. In column 31 of the section entitled "Ishtar and Izdubar," according to Leonidas Le Cenci Hamilton's translation of 1884, the king summons his seers and commands them to interpret a troubling dream that he has had, whereupon:

> *The seers in silence stand, perplexed and think ...*
> *And they now prostrate fall before his throne,*

Interpreting Dreams

"Forgive thy seers!" one cries, "O mighty One!
For we this dreadful dream do fear portends
Thy harm! A god some message to thee sends!
We know not what, but fear for thee."

A similar story is told in the Old Testament Book of Daniel (2:2-3), which relates that King Nebuchadnezzar: "commanded to call the magicians, and the astrologers, and the sorcerers, and the Chaldeans, for to shew the king his dreams. So they came and stood before the king. And the king said unto them, I have dreamed a dream, and my spirit was troubled to know the dream." In the end it was Daniel, who, enlightened by a vision sent to him by God, interpreted Nebuchadnezzar 's dream, first explaining: "The secret which the king hath demanded cannot the wise men, the astrologers, the magicians, the soothsayers, shew unto the king; But there is a God in heaven that revealeth secrets, and maketh known to the king Nebuchadnezzar what shall be in the latter days." (Daniel 2 27-28).

From these two pieces of evidence alone, we can conclude that nearly two millennia ago, dreams were taken extremely seriously as important portents, or messages, from a divine source, whose interpretation required equally divine inspiration or guidance.

Throughout the history of humankind, numerous tribes and civilizations have credited dreams with having an external cause. It was once almost universally believed that nightmares, for instance, were inflicted on defenceless sleepers by devils, demons, and other malevolent spirits, while enjoyable dreams were said to have their origins in benevolent supernatural beings. (This outlook is embodied in the concepts underlying the dreamcatcher—essentially a webbed hoop that resembles a spider's web or decorated tennis racket—that, in Native American tradition, is hung by a child's bed in order to trap, and thus fend off, bad dreams, while at the same time enabling happiness-infused dreams to enter the young sleeper's slumber.)

Other cultures have regarded dreamland as being a sort of parallel universe that only becomes accessible to us when we lose consciousness. In Hudson Bay, for example, some Inuit people hold that our souls temporarily leave our bodies while we are sleeping, and that we are witnessing their adventures as we dream. Likewise, some "New Age" theorists maintain that it is during sleep that the phenomena known as out-of-body experiences (O.B.E.s), astral projection, or astral travel, occur, when our disembodied spirits slip away from our cumbersome bodies (to which they remain harnessed by a silver cord, however) to travel freely through time and space. Although few Westerners today are superstitious or unconventional enough to believe that dreams are literal omens or manifestations of real events, most of us would probably accept that they are not without personal meaning.

Some researchers propose that dreams are a kind of side effect of the re-experiencing, sorting, and consequent forgetting or laying-down of memories that the brain undertakes during its "downtime," or sleep, a rational and compelling hypothesis that it would be difficult to reject out of hand.

Yet this does not explain why, as commonly happens, we may go to sleep mulling over a conundrum and awake in possession of a neat solution, one that came to us in a dream. Nor does it account for the delightful dreams that may hearten us in times of trouble, or for the recurring dreams that may plague our sleep, or for the absurd dream storylines, incongruous characters, and out-of-character behaviour to which we may be party while we are sleeping. And if, as is sometimes claimed, dreams are merely muddled memories, why can they affect us so powerfully? "I've dreamt in my life dreams that have stayed with me ever after, and changed my ideas; they've gone through and through me, like wine through water, and altered the colour of my mind." Why do Emily Brontë's words, immortalized in her novel *Wuthering Heights* (1847), ring so true?

The Interpretation of Dreams

The rejection of superstitious beliefs in favour of scientific ones, and the consequent search for a physiological or psychological prompt for our dreams, was initiated several centuries before the birth of Christ by such Greek philosophers as Heraclitus (*c.*544–483 B.C.), Plato (*c.*427–347 B.C.), and Aristotle (384–322 B.C.), along with Hippocrates (*c.*460–377 B.C.), the "father of medicine." And it was a Roman work, *Oneirocriticon (The Interpretation of Dreams), by Artemidorus* (A.D. 138–180), that was probably the first dream "dictionary" of the symbol-based, self-help type with which we are familiar today. All of these thinkers proposed that our dreams originate within ourselves, and that while certain of their elements may be common to humankind, their meaning is largely personal, in that they arise from, and pertain to, the dreamer's individual circumstances.

Although many wise words about dreams were subsequently penned by poets, playwrights, novelists, and essayists—an example being William Hazlitt's astute observation "We are not hypocrites in our sleep" ("On Dreams," *The Plain Speaker*, 1826)—and the Romantic movement of the nineteenth century kindled a renewed, albeit somewhat vague, interest in the subject, it was not until the twentieth century that dreams again attracted serious, and sustained, general attention. That they then did so, and that research into dreams and their possible meanings has, a century later, developed into a significant field of scientific study, is largely due to Sigmund Freud (1865–1939), the Austrian "father of psychoanalysis" whose seminal work *Die Traumdeutung (The Interpretation of Dreams)* caused a sensation when it was first published in 1900. "In the following pages, I shall demonstrate that there is a psychological technique which makes it possible to interpret dreams, and that on the application of this technique, every dream will reveal itself as a psychological structure, full of significance, and one which may be assigned to a specific place in the psychic activities of the waking state." The dry opening words of *The Interpretation of Dreams may have seemed* innocuous, but they introduced ideas so radical, and so shocking to the buttoned-up sensibilities of the pre–World War I era, that they earned their author widespread notoriety. Freud proposed the theory that the human psyche comprises the superego, or conscience; the ego, or the conscious, "civilized" mind; and the id, or the nebulous realm of unconscious, "uncivilized" thoughts. While we are awake, the ego—despite being subject to modification by the superego—is essentially in control, perhaps its most important task being to suppress the "animal" urges, "antisocial" instincts, and sensory quest for self-gratification that emanate from the id. It does this in order to ensure that we behave conventionally and, as a result, fit in with, and are accepted by, the society in which we live. When we are asleep, however, the ego loosens its stranglehold on the id, enabling these "animal" urges and "antisocial" instincts to float to the surface of our sleeping minds, albeit usually disguised in symbolic form, thereby preventing the conscious mind from instantly recognizing the nature of "the beast" and being shocked into wakefulness and the resumption of its repressive function.

What really repelled the "respectable," strait-laced readers of *The Interpretation of Dreams was Freud's proposition* that the ego is constantly trying to quash the frequently amoral or even incestuous sexual drives and desires to which we have been longing to give free rein since infancy, and that it is these that are expressed, and that may find fulfilment, in our dreams. A very simplified summing-up of the Freudian view of dreams is therefore that they are wish-fulfilment fantasies that often focus on the gratification of the libido, but not overtly so, so that it is necessary to interpret the dream's manifest content, or symbolism, in order to reveal its latent content, or the truth. Freud believed that certain symbols were favoured by the id in all of us: phallic symbols, for example: "It is quite unmistakable that all weapons and tools are used as symbols for the male organ: e.g., ploughshare, hammer, gun, revolver, dagger, sword, etc." (*ibid*). Yet while acknowledging our unconscious propensity to "dream up" the same types of symbols, Freud did not consider dreams to be concerned with anything more than personal wish fulfilment.

Although twenty-first-century dream researchers and psychoanalysts respect and admire Freud for his groundbreaking work, most would not unreservedly endorse his theories. For while the Freudian viewpoint is certainly worthy of consideration, the modern consensus is that dreams should be examined from at least the Jungian angle as well. Their differences— first minor, but eventually unbridgeable—may eventually have driven these erstwhile colleagues to part ways, but today the joint legacies of Freud and the Swiss analytical psychologist Carl Jung (1875–1961) are regarded as the twin pillars on which a century's worth of dream-interpretation theories and practice have been constructed.

Given their brief collaboration, it is not, perhaps, surprising that many of Jung's ideas are comparable to those of Freud. He, too, surmised that the human psyche consists of three levels, for instance, but deviated from Freud by identifying them as being the conscious mind, which regulates our waking thoughts; the personal unconscious, the realm of impulses that are unique to us as individuals; and the collective unconscious, effectively a repository of humankind's memories, experiences, and instincts, which we have inherited from our common ancestors and often take the form of archetypes, or universal symbols (see the chapter on Archetypal and Symbolic Figures for a more detailed discussion of some of these). "I was never able to agree with Freud that the dream is a 'façade' behind which its meaning lies hidden—a meaning already known, but maliciously, so to speak, withheld from consciousness..." stated Jung in *Memories, Dreams, Reflections* (1962). Nor did he share Freud's conclusion that dreams were primarily concerned with wish fulfilment. Instead, Jung believed that dreams are therapeutic tools initiated by the self, or each human's psychic "core," with the purpose of trying to achieve individuation— "wholeness," or the perfect balance of the conscious and unconscious parts of our psyche.

It is usually only when we are asleep that the unconscious—personal and collective—is able to express itself without interference by the conscious mind, and the dreams that flow from it, Jung averred, "give information about the secrets of the inner life and reveal to the dreamer hidden factors of his personality" ("Dream-Analysis," *Modern Man in Search of a Soul*, 1933). Jung believed that when the conscious mind reasserts itself and we leave *dreamland* and awaken, we should consequently consciously try to understand the dream messages generated by the unconscious mind, which "harbours no intention to deceive, but expresses something as best it can," often in the form of personal or archetypal symbols. In short, if you can comprehend the language of your unconscious, and are willing to heed what it is telling you, chances are that you will become a more balanced and happier individual.

The Freudian View of Dreams as Wish Fulfillment

"The ancient belief that dreams reveal the future is not indeed entirely devoid of truth. By representing a wish as fulfilled the dream certainly leads us into the future; but this future, which the dreamer accepts as his present, has been shaped in the likeness of the past by the indestructible wish."

Sigmund Freud, *The Interpretation of Dreams* (1900)

The Jungian View of Dreams and the Unconscious

'The view that dreams are merely imaginary fulfillments of suppressed wishes has long since been superseded. It is certainly true that there are dreams which embody suppressed wishes and fears, but what is there which the dream cannot on occasion embody? Dreams may give expression to ineluctable truths, to philosophical pronouncements, illusions, wild fantasies, memories, plans, anticipations, irrational experiences, even telepathic visions, and heaven knows what besides. One thing we ought never to forget: almost the half of our lives is passed in a more or less unconscious state. The dream is specifically the utterance of the unconscious. We may call consciousness the daylight realm of the human psyche, and contrast it with the nocturnal realm of unconscious psychic activity which we apprehend as dreamlike fantasy. It is certain that consciousness consist not only of wishes and fears, but of vastly more than these, and it is highly probable that the unconscious psyche contains a wealth of contents and living forms equal to or even greater than does consciousness, which is characterized by concentration, limitation and exclusion.'

—Carl Jung "Dream-Analysis," *Modern Man in Search of a Soul* (1933)

Types of Dream

Look through the body of research that is today available to anyone interested in dreams, and it soon becomes evident that dreams can be classified into a number of common types or categories, including the following:

> literal, factual, and processing dreams
> physiological and punning dreams
> problem-solving and inspirational dreams
> cathartic and safety-valve dreams
> contrary, compensatory, or wish-fulfillment dreams
> recurring dreams
> nightmares
> precognitive and telepathic dreams

About Our Dreams

Because you are likely to experience at least some of these types of dreams, you may find it useful to know a little about the form that they typically take and their possible causes. Note that dream types may also overlap, so that a nightmare in which you are struggling to breathe may also be a recurring dream, as well as a literal and physiological one, if, for example, your bedroom is constantly and grossly overheated.

Literal, Factual, and Processing Dreams

Literal and factual dreams reflect reality, or, as the Indian poet Rabindranath Tagore so elegantly put it, "In the drowsy dark cave of the mind / dreams build their nest with fragments / dropped from the day's caravan" (*Fireflies*, 1928). They can be concerned with the past, present, or future, although processing dreams, as literal and factual dreams are sometimes also called, are generally more concerned with the reexperiencing and digesting of memories. If you went to sleep at the end of a day spent shopping and dreamed of revisiting the same stores in which you had just spent real time, you experienced a literal, factual, or processing dream. If you dreamed that someone was knocking insistently on your bedroom door, and then awoke to find that this was indeed the case, you also had a literal, or factual, dream. And if you were mulling over the prospect of the many errands that you had to run the next day before losing consciousness and abandoning yourself to sleep, and then found yourself performing some of these chores in dreamland, your dream again falls into the literal or factual category.

Researchers generally do not consider such dreams to have hidden or especially significant meanings, but believe that they may highlight the dreamer's preoccupations, and may also be part of the process by which the brain recalls and reappraises its memories of the day before either jettisoning or preserving them.

Physiological and Punning Dreams

Physiological dreams are those that reflect the state of the dreamer's body. If, for example, you went to bed dehydrated, and then became increasingly parched as the night progressed, your actual thirst may have intruded into your dream, perhaps manifesting itself as a longing for a long, cool drink of refreshing water as you endured a hot and dry dreamland atmosphere. Or maybe your bedding obstructed your nose and mouth as you slept, prompting a physiological dream in which you were being suffocated by someone and were gasping desperately for breath.

Researchers are divided about whether physiological dreams can reveal as yet undiagnosed internal problems. Some might say that a dream of an army of white-clothed ants battling against a horde of black aphids could depict, in symbolic form, the body's white blood cells struggling to vanquish the threat posed by a cancerous tumor that has started to develop within the dreamer's body. Others would dismiss this interpretation as being either fanciful (particularly if no tumor is subsequently diagnosed), coincidence (if it later is), or merely a reflection of the dreamer's health concerns or hypochondria, whether or not cancer subsequently rears its ugly head in the real world. There is currently no proof either way, so if you are troubled by a recurring dream that you believe may refer to your health, asking your doctor to check you over may at the very least put your mind at rest, thereby enabling you to enjoy a good night's sleep.

Punning dreams are not always also physiological dreams, but puns (plays on words) are often used in dreams as apt metaphors for how we are feeling. In such dreams, puns may be expressed in speech or writing, or they may be acted out. During a period in my life when I was so overwhelmed by working demands that there was no time at all for relaxation, I dreamed, for example, of keeling over every time that I stood up, while despairingly wailing "I've lost my balance!" for good measure. On waking, it was obvious to me that my dream referred to the loss of my usually healthy work–life balance in the waking world, which I was consciously trying to disregard in order to meet my deadlines. Similarly, if your waking hours are spent in a way that you find distasteful, and you dreamed of vomiting uncontrollably, your unconscious may have been graphically portraying your real-life sense of being "sickened," or of being made to feel "sick to the stomach," by your waking circumstances. Or if you dreamed of watching a dog slink into its kennel, a miserable expression on its face and its tail tucked abjectly between its legs as its owner berated it for having misbehaved, could the unconscious reference have been to the guilt that you feel for having cheated on your partner, and your sense of being "in the doghouse" now that he or she's discovered what you've been up to?

Punning dreams can—maybe incidentally, maybe not—also paint such ludicrous pictures that your conscious self can't help but smile at their memory, thereby lightening the negative mood that may have given rise to them. The Russian composer Igor Stravinsky (1882–1971) obviously felt aggrieved that unsympathetic music critics apparently "shut their ears" to his works, but cannot have taken them too seriously following his dream, reported in the English newspaper *The Evening Standard*, on October 29, 1969, that they "were small and rodent-like with padlocked ears, as if they had stepped out of a painting by Goya."

Problem-solving and Inspirational Dreams

If no solution immediately springs to mind when we are faced with a dilemma, or are pondering an important decision or course of action, we may decide to "sleep on it." Having literally "slept on it," we may then wake up with a clear idea of how best to resolve our difficulties or of how best to proceed. Most researchers agree that problem-solving dreams, and sometimes also inspirational dreams, emanate from deep within our unconscious minds in response to a conundrum that the conscious mind has been unable to solve. Remember that although we distinguish our thought processes by labeling them as being "conscious" or "unconscious," "waking" or "dreaming," "reasoning" or "intuitive," all are generated by your brain, and all are therefore fundamentally "on your side." If you have been consciously preoccupied with a problem during your waking hours, it stands to reason that it has concerned you on an unconscious level, too, so that when you finally enter the realm of your unconscious in your dreams, you may find that the solution is waiting for you there, albeit maybe disguised as a symbol.

There are a number of famous examples of problem-solving dreams, and at least two have resulted in inventions that continue to play an important role in everyday life the world over. Ball-bearings, for instance, are said to have been invented by the Scottish engineer James Watt (1736–1819) as a result of his recurring dreams of being battered by a hailstorm of lead pellets, which eventually led him to realize that molten lead will form spheres if dropped from a significant height. And the idea for setting the lockstitch sewing-machine needle's hole in its tip, rather than its end, is said to have come to U.S. inventor Elias Howe (1819–67) following a dream of tribesmen armed with spears that had pierced blades. Both of these inventions represented important breakthroughs to the men who had dreamed them up.

Problem-solving dreams can thus also be inspirational dreams, but inspirational dreams do not always arise in response to a waking-life problem. Whatever their cause, these types of dreams can have the most magical consequences for humankind. The haunting refrains that have permeated the dreams of distinguished musicians have sometimes lingered long enough to be captured on paper, a dream of Satan playing the violin, for example, in the case of the Italian composer and violinist Guiseppe Tartini (1692–1770) resulting in *The Devil's Trill* sonata of 1714.

Cathartic and Safety-Valve Dreams

If you dreamed that you told someone—perhaps a forbidding figure of absolute authority in your waking world—what you really think of them, beat them up, or otherwise asserted yourself aggressively or violently over them, you may have woken up feeling rather shocked by your dreamland actions. But if you also experienced a sense of release or relief, you probably had a cathartic or safety-valve dream. For if, during your waking hours, you have to accede to that person's will without question, you may have been feeling increasingly resentful of having to submit to the power that he or she wields over you. In this case, you may have been longing to reverse your respective positions so that you are the one who is in control and able to punish your erstwhile tormentor. By allowing you to do just that in the parallel world of dreamland, your dream may have enabled you to let off steam, thus perhaps heading off a similar (although probably less aggressive) outburst or attack that may otherwise have occurred had your pent-up frustrations boiled over in real life, with, no doubt, disastrous consequences.

Contrary, Compensatory or Wish-fulfillment Dreams

Freudians would say that cathartic and safety-valve dreams are also wish-fulfillment dreams because they give the instincts of the id (our unconscious) an outlet, thereby fulfilling "base" desires that the ego, regarding them as being socially unacceptable, generally successfully suppresses. They could equally be classed as contrary or compensatory dreams because they reverse, or are completely contrary to, one's real-life situation and thus compensate, albeit only in dreamland, for unsatisfactory waking conditions.

Our contrary, compensatory, or wish-fulfillment dreams can give us a much-needed emotional high when our real-world circumstances are making us feel low and hopeless, which may be why we dream them up. If, for example, you are going through a period of relative poverty and spend your waking hours anxiously trying to devise ways of reducing your outgoings, you probably woke with a smile on your face after a dream in which you won a million dollars on the lottery and had a wonderful time splashing out on frivolous fripperies without even asking their price. Similarly, if you have secretly always longed to be an astronaut, but know that realizing your dream is out of the question in the real world, dreaming of zipping yourself into a spacesuit, taking your place on a space shuttle, and counting down the seconds to blast-off would be your unconscious mind's way of granting you your dream and boosting your morale.

Wishful thinking may therefore be rewarded with wish fulfillment in dreamland, but, according to Jung, there may be another, less clear-cut, reason why we have compensatory dreams—particularly if they paint a negative dreamland picture—and that is to achieve, or maintain, a balanced psyche.

> The psyche is a self-regulating system that maintains itself in equilibrium as the body does. Every process that goes too far immediately and inevitably calls forth a compensatory activity. Without such adjustments a normal metabolism would not exist, nor would the normal psyche ... The relationship between conscious and unconscious is compensatory. This fact ... affords a rule for dream interpretation. It is always helpful, when we set out to interpret a dream, to ask: What conscious attitude does it compensate?
> —Jung, "Dream-Analysis," *ibid.*

According to this theory, if, for example, you are beset by crippling shyness in the waking world, your dreaming self may be transformed into a sparkling, super-confident, social butterfly. So if you find yourself puzzling over the possible meaning of a dream in which you behaved totally out of character, remember to take compensation into consideration

Recurring Dreams

Recurring dreams need not be identical in content, but the dream theme will usually be broadly consistent. If you often dream of competing in a race, of struggling to climb to the summit of a mountain, or of being humiliated by your classmates, for instance, the finer details of your dreamland experience may change, but the central feeling remains the same. No doubt the same is true of the emotional response that it elicits from your dreaming self.

Recurring dreams may or may not be anxiety dreams or nightmares. Psychologists believe, though, that they are generally dreams that provoke a profoundly negative reaction in us. They may be unconscious expressions of our deepest worries, fears, or memories. Sometimes these arouse such a powerful response in us that we push them to the back of our conscious minds because we find them so painful, uncomfortable, or embarrassing to confront. And because we have not consciously faced and worked them through, they continue to lurk in the depths of our unconscious, surfacing during our sleep in the form of recurring dreams. If you suffer from upsetting recurring dreams, putting a stop to them may therefore require some bravery on your part (see the following section on nightmares for further advice).

Nightmares

Nightmares prove that many of our fears are "all in the mind," for if you think about it rationally, a dream is an intangible that can cause you no harm and is therefore nothing to be afraid of. But if that is the case, why do we sometimes wake up with a start, with a dry mouth, a racing heart, in a sweat, and on occasions even screaming?

The answer lies in whatever it is that we consciously fear, or that makes us feel exceptionally anxious, and that we therefore do our best to avoid or not to think about when we are awake. That consciously ignored fear remains dormant in our unconscious mind, however, and because we can exert little, if any, conscious control over dreamland, the province of the unconscious, it may come to the fore when activated by a certain trigger that we have encountered during the day. The trigger may be a stressful situation, an upsetting memory, or the arousal of a phobia: encountering a spider in the waking world may give rise to a nightmare about being entrapped by a monstrous spider if, for instance, you are an arachnophobic. But what if you are not at all bothered by spiders in the real world, yet your dreaming self was scared witless by a nocturnal encounter by a sinister black-widow spider? If you are determined to get to the bottom of a bad dream like this, it may help to ask yourself what the black widow could have represented, such as a predatory older woman who, if you are a younger man, you may have sensed has amorous designs on you, and who you fear may "eat you for breakfast" should you fall into her clutches.

If a spider, monster, ogre, or demon terrorized you while you were sleeping, remember that it was your unconscious, in other words, you, that conjured it up, and that, in the words of Jung, "The unconscious is not a demonic monster, but a thing of nature that is perfectly neutral as far as moral sense, esthetic taste and intellectual judgement go. It is dangerous only when our conscious attitude to it becomes hopelessly false. And this danger grows in the measure that we practice repressions. But as soon as the patient begins to assimilate the contents that were previously unconscious, the danger from the side of the unconscious diminishes." ("Dream-Analysis," *ibid.*)

Whatever it is that you decide that your menacing monster may have symbolized, most therapists would concur with Jung that the only really effective way of banishing it from your dreams for good is consciously to address it and to think about why you relate or respond to it in such an extreme manner. By making an effort to understand what it represents and why this has the power to frighten you so, you will, it is hoped, demystify the monster that terrorizes you in the darker depths of dreamland, gain control over your fear, and thus neutralize the threat that it poses to your psychic wellbeing. "Knowledge is power," it is said, and this is often especially true when you are able to pluck up the courage to confront your bogeymen or unresolved issues, whereupon you may see them for the pathetic things that they actually are, enabling you to overcome your fear and leave it behind you, in the past, as you move confidently on into the future. Be warned that this process is rarely quickly or easily accomplished, however, and if you regularly suffer from terrible nightmares, seeking the help of a trained therapist may be a wise strategy.

Precognitive and Telepathic Dreams

Now that scientific principles have been overwhelmingly applied to the study and analysis of dreams, the notion that we may receive psychic omens foretelling future events, or telepathic communications from others—be they hale and hearty, sick or dying, or even long dead—in our dreams is generally dismissed out of hand. And should an event that was apparently foreseen in a precognitive, prophetic, or clairvoyant dream actually come to pass in the real world, the explanation is usually put down either to coincidence or to an unconscious recognition of the inevitability of the event occurring. If you dreamed of crashing your automobile and later really did so, for example, the suggestion would be that you'd unconsciously picked up clues that your automobile's brakes were faulty and that there was consequently an accident "waiting to happen."

No one can yet claim to understand the workings of the human mind fully, however. And there have been many well-documented instances of individuals dreaming of disasters occurring on different continents that have later come to pass, as well as of people being visited by a loved one, or of hearing a message from a significant someone, in dreamland shortly before receiving news of their actual demise at around that very time. So if you strongly feel that you have had a precognitive or telepathic dream, you may well be right. If you think that this may indeed be the case, make sure that you record the details of your dream as fully as possible, along with the date (and if you can, also note down the time) on which you dreamed your portentous dream, so that you later have proof should the events of your dream really be played out in the waking world. Do not panic on waking from such an unsettling dream, however, because unless you already know that you have psychic abilities, a dreamland fantasy, or else unconscious knowledge, will still be the most likely explanation for it.

Decoding Your Dreams

You may not think that you dream at all, but be assured that you do. If you awake with no memory of having dreamed, it may either be that the details of the night's dreams have been driven from your conscious mind by over-riding thoughts of what the new day will bring or that you woke at the "wrong" time during the sleep cycle.

Unless you suffer from insomnia or another type of sleep disturbance, you will usually spend the bulk of your night in "slow-wave" sleep, of which there are four distinct stages.

Drifting off to sleep is the first stage, when your body and brain relax (sometimes triggering myoclonic jerks, or involuntary muscular spasms), your eyes roll, and you enter the hypnagogic state, during which you may see and hear random visions and voices. You do not dream during this stage, however.

During the second stage, you sink ever deeper into unconsciousness, but still aren't truly asleep, nor are you dreaming.

By the time that you enter the third stage, when you are at last fast asleep, you will have become utterly relaxed, but are still not dreaming.

The fourth stage of sleep is known as orthodox, or nonrapid-eye-movement (N.R.E.M.), sleep, when your unconscious mind has come to the fore and your brain arranges for any damage to your body or breaches of your immune system to be repaired, also, it is thought, addressing the day's memories. Although you may be hit by night terrors, or unspecific feelings of dread, during this stage of sleep, these are not technically dreams.

It typically takes between ninety and one hundred minutes to pass through the four stages of slow-wave sleep, when your brainwaves are pulsing at their slowest rate and your vital functions have also slowed considerably, after which you move backward through the cycle, and then forward again.

You will probably have noted that dreams do not feature in any of the four stages of slow-wave sleep, so when exactly do you dream? The answer is after you have returned to the first stage, at which point you enter paradoxical, or rapid-eye-movement (R.E.M.), sleep, when your brainwaves and body functions quicken and your eyeballs flit around behind your closed eyelids. If you awake from a vivid dream now, you may not be able to move, for while the unconscious sends you off on dreamland adventures, it also takes the precaution of paralyzing you to prevent you from acting out the dramatic action of your dream in reality.

About Our Dreams

Your first taste of the R.E.M., or dreaming, phase of sleeps lasts for only around ten minutes before you reembark on the four stages of the slow-wave sleep cycle again, but each R.E.M. period—and they average four a night—gradually lengthens so that the ultimate, and longest, phase of dreams that you may experience can last for about forty-five minutes. And it is the dreams that occur during this final incidence, as you increasingly surface into consciousness, that you are most likely to remember.

Like Samuel Taylor Coleridge, you too may already be aware of how quickly the details of your dreams elude your powers of recall once you have woken up and started your early morning ritual. If you're serious about analysing your dreams, this is why it's important to record them before your conscious thoughts of the day's "to-do" list, or that first shot of caffeine, crowd out your ephemeral memories of events in dreamland. Capture your dreams as soon as you awake, before you get up, either by dictating them into your phone's voice memo function or another recording device, or by scribbling them into a notebook (depending on your preferred method, remember to keep your device or a pen, paper, and perhaps also a flashlight, to hand by your bedside).

Once you have recorded the crucial details, note the date, because this may later help you to identify a waking-world trigger or a real-time pattern to your dreams. (You'll also find a space on each of the dream-subject pages that follows on which to jot down the gist of a relevant dream.) It may be, for instance, that studying your dream diary reveals that in December you invariably have disturbing dreams about family arguments, or that you consistently dreamed of inheriting a fortune at a time when money was particularly tight. It's particularly important that you log the atmosphere of your dream and how your dreaming self felt, for emotions prevail in dreamland, and will almost certainly provide you with the key to decoding your dreams.

Having acted as a human dreamcatcher while muzzily cocooned in your warm, cozy bed, you can then set the day under way and get on with the business of living life in the real world. Later on, when you have some free time, solitude, and emotional distance, you'll be able to pick up where you left off and consciously consider your dream when your thoughts are unclouded by emotive residual memories. Sometimes the message conveyed by your dream will be crystal clear. On other occasions, you may find the advice in this book enlightening as you grope your way toward settling on a likely interpretation. And if you are on the verge of giving up because you find a dream utterly baffling, you may find it helpful to use such Freudian tricks as free association, or writing down every little thing that springs to mind when you think of a particular aspect of your dream, without giving it a second's thought. Or you might try Jungian techniques like direct association, or focusing intensely on a dream symbol and listing everything with which you associate it; or any other interpretive strategy, such as teasing out possibly significant considerations by interviewing yourself (for instance, "Did the way that the gray cat in your dream looked or behaved remind you of anyone or anything?")

The Talmud (Berakhot 55a) asserts that "A dream that is not interpreted is like a letter that has not been opened." Think about the life-changing messages that have been mailed to you in the real world: a declaration of love; news of an exam success or failure; of a birth; of an invitation to attend a job interview; of someone's proposed visit. It matters not who you believe the sender of your dreams to be—be it a divine agency, or your own, unconscious mind—but can you afford to remain ignorant of the potentially illuminating, if not life-altering, communiqués that are delivered to you in your sleep?

Part 2:
The Dreams and
their Meanings

The Body

If you are consciously troubled by a niggling feeling that all is not well with your health, and you had a worrying dream that appeared to confirm your worst fears, your unconscious may merely have been providing an outlet for the worries that your conscious mind is trying to quash. (And if such dreams are recurring, consulting your doctor may give you peace of mind.) It is more likely, however, that your unconscious seized on and portrayed a pun as a way of expressing your current state of mind.

Beauty and Ugliness

As much as we may try to counter such beliefs in the waking world, in the world of dreams, concepts of beauty and ugliness are not always skin-deep: they are often representative of our hopes, fears, and feelings about the inner character of ourselves and others.

Symbolic and Verbal Associations

› Aspirations for the admiration and approval of others
› Fears about growing older; physical aging
› Our hopes and fears about the character of ourselves and others
› Revulsion, or being repulsed; moral repulsion
› Harboring unhealthy or "ugly" emotions, or behaving in an obnoxious manner

Positive Interpretations: The image that we present to others, or the persona that we show to the world, is often represented in our dreams by a focus on the appearance of our physical self. If, in your dream, you

37

looked into the mirror to see a vision of exquisite loveliness, it may be that this is how you want the world to see you. Do you wish for others to admire you for your beautiful appearance or moral character? Or did you have a dream in which someone else's physical beauty caused you to have feelings of yearning, attraction, or admiration? If this is the case, it may be that your dream self has encountered your anima (if you are a man) or animus (if you are a woman): a character who is the mirror image, or reverse, of your soul, and whose appearance in your dream may indicate the need for balance in your waking life. If you are a man, it may signal that it is time for you to get in touch with your emotional, intuitive, or empathetic side. Conversely, if you are a woman, the appearance of your animus may be your unconscious mind's way of prompting you to become more intellectually focused, practical, or confident.

Negative Interpretations: If you had a dream in which you looked into the mirror to find that your body had become twisted and ugly, could it be that you are harboring an "ugly" emotion, such as jealousy or envy, and that you are worried that others may "see" this in you and find you repulsive? Alternatively, if your dream self was horrified to see that you had become old and wrinkled, this may be your unconscious expression of your fears and/or regrets about the physical effects associated with aging. But if you were terrified, horrified, or revolted by someone else's ugliness in your dream, do you know who the person was? Your dreaming image of them may indicate that this person is—by means of their actions or their intentions—somehow plaguing you during waking hours, or that their attitude or their "energy" is repulsive to you in some way. The dream meanings associated with the relative beauty or ugliness of the specific body parts will be addressed in detail, one by one, in later sections of this book.

Blood and Guts

Because we don't usually see someone's blood unless they have been injured—and because, if a person loses enough blood, they are likely to die—the letting of blood in dreamland is often a powerful symbol of the life force ebbing from someone. Similar interpretations can be applied to a dream that focuses on intestines (either our own or someone else's)—though, depending on the context, there are a number of other explanations that should be considered.

Symbolic and Verbal Associations

› Mortality; the "life force"
› Menstruation; pregnancy
› Injury, or loss of vitality
› "Bleeding someone dry"
› Coming to terms with, "stomaching," or "digesting" new information
› Courage, or "having the guts" to do something

Positive Interpretations: If you are a woman of childbearing age and you had a dream that featured or spotlighted blood, then your unconscious may be honing in on your hopes or fears about pregnancy. Otherwise, it may just be that you are about to begin menstruating. However, if you had a dream in which you received a life-saving blood transfusion, you should think about who the person was who either administered the transfusion or donated the blood; perhaps he or she has the ability to revitalize or heal you in some way in the waking world.

Negative Interpretations: If you had a dream in which you were chopping up carrots for dinner and suddenly chopped into your finger by mistake, or if you dreamed that you were more seriously injured, perhaps that you were attacked and stabbed by someone, then your dream self's loss of blood may be representative of your feelings of having lost vitality in the real world. Could it be that you have been overworking yourself in order to finish the new addition on your house by the holidays? Or has someone else, perhaps an overly needy friend or relative, been wearing you down or "sapping your strength"? If you dreamed that your child knifed you in the belly, is he "bleeding you dry" in the waking world through his ceaseless demands for your time or money? Perhaps not so symbolic, a dream of intestinal pain could simply mean that you ate too much (or not enough) food for dinner and that you are suffering for it during your slumbering hours. Or is it that your unconscious is telling you that you are feeling "starved" of love or affection? If this is not the case, however, you might want to ask yourself whether you are finding it difficult to "stomach" or "digest" something in real life, such as your widowed mother having taken on a new boyfriend. Alternatively, could it be that you have been lacking the "guts" to do something in the real world, such as quitting the job that you hate?

Bodily Functions

It's not a pleasant subject, in most people's opinion, but such bodily functions as urination and defecation do serve the important purpose of ridding our bodies of waste. And when we dream of ourselves performing these functions, the meaning is likely to be similar, though the dream probably has to do with the elimination of emotional matter, such as unpleasant memories.

Symbolic and Verbal Associations

› Elimination of emotional waste
› "Letting go" of unhealthy feelings or the past
› Emotional "blockage" or constipation; "anal retention"
› Cleanliness versus filth or foulness
› Being emotionally in, or out of, control

Positive Interpretations: A dream in which you found yourself urinating or defecating is likely to signify the need for an emotional purging of some sort, whether it is an unpleasant memory that you need to let go of or a past lesson that you have learned and can now put behind you, so that it may no longer trouble your mind So, if you found your dream self frantically racing to get to the bathroom, and then finally emerging with relief, you may need to ask yourself if it is time to "flush out" your emotional system during waking hours. Have you felt that you have been emotionally burdened of late? Perhaps a recent visit to your hometown has caused your mind to be troubled by the memory of an argument that you had with your now deceased father? Or do you long to rid yourself of your jealous feelings toward your best friend, who has recently been promoted to an executive position within her company? Whatever the cause of the dream, it is likely that it was your unconscious mind's way of signalling to you that you would be happier if you were to dedicate yourself to performing some serious emotional purging.

Negative Interpretations: Did your dream self have difficulties due to constipation? Or perhaps your dreaming mind cast you in a scenario in which you suffered from diarrhea? An analysis of the dream situation should give you a clue as to whether you have been emotionally "blocked," constipated, or "anally retentive," or, alternatively, whether you have lately spun out of control in the emotional arena of your waking world. Or perhaps your dream self was desperately searching for a public restroom, only to look in vain, or to find one that was all locked up and to which you could not gain access. If this was the case, it may be that your waking self needs to find the key, or the catalyst, for a much-needed emotional release. In another scenario, if you had a dream in which you or your belongings were fouled by someone else's urine or feces, do you know who the person was? You may want to consider whether you have been taken advantage of or "dumped on" by this person.

Ears & Hearing

As hearing is one of the major senses that most people rely upon for taking in information, communicating, and navigating their way through the world, it is no wonder that there are so many symbolic associations and expressions relating to the organs with which we hear: the ears.

Symbolic and Verbal Associations

› Keeping an "ear to the ground," or staying alert or informed
› Focusing one's attention, or being "all ears"
› Not listening, or "closing one's ears," to the truth
› Ignoring, or "turning a deaf ear" to, what someone is saying
› "Wagging ears"; the circulation of gossip
› "Burning ears": sensing that someone is talking or gossiping behind one's back
› Being "up to one's ears," i.e., overburdened or fully occupied

Positive Interpretations: Hearing, or "listening out," is an important, primary way detecting things to come—both literally and figuratively—in the waking world. Did your dreaming mind cast you in a situation in which you were bent down, listening intently, with an "ear to the ground"? If so, then this could be an unconscious clue that you need to stay alert and informed about what is happening around you in the waking world—perhaps at work, where an upcoming company reorganization may lead to promotions and/or layoffs. Alternatively, a dream that focuses on your (or someone else's) ear may be a signal that you need to pay more attention to the things that people are telling you. In another scenario, if you had a dream in which someone's ears had grown to an extraordinary size, you may want to consider whether that person is "all ears" or ready to hear something that you have been wanting to tell them for some time.

Negative Interpretations: If you dreamed that you were deaf or hard of hearing, and if you do not suffer from hearing problems in the waking world, could it be that you have been "closing your ears" to some hard truth that you haven't wanted to hear in the waking world? In your dream, did you know the person who was trying to speak to you? Do they have some information that may be difficult—yet important—for you to "hear"? Alternatively, if you dreamed that someone else had gone deaf, has that person been "turning a deaf ear" to, or ignoring, something that you have been telling (or asking of) them in the waking world? Having a dream that places the focus on "wagging" or "burning" ears may be your unconscious mind's way of telling you that it is possible that someone you know has been gossiping or talking behind your back. Or is it you who has been doing the gossiping? The specific dream scenario involved, and your dreaming reaction to it, should give you a clue as to how to interpret your dream.

Eyes and Eyesight

We often hear people say that the eyes are the "windows to the soul," which is, perhaps, an allusion to the eyes' crucial function in communicating and relaying emotions. The eyes, the organs of sight, have long been the subject of countless songs and stories, and when they feature in our dreams, the meaning can be as rich and multilayered as the ancient symbolism that surrounds these all-important organs.

Symbolic and Verbal Associations

› "Having an eye" or "having eyes" for (liking, being interested in, or having a flair for) someone or something
› Agreeing, or "seeing eye to eye"
› "Windows to the soul"
› The "third eye"; insight
› "Avoiding eye contact," or guilty behavior
› Looking at things in a skewed, or "cock-eyed" fashion
› "Turning a blind eye" or "closing one's eyes," to the truth
› Being near or short-sighted; lacking imagination or insight
› The "green-eyed monster," jealousy

Positive Interpretations: If you had a dream that focused on someone's eye color, you may begin to understand its meaning by considering the color of the person's eyes and how it made you feel about him or her. For instance, did your dream emphasize the innocence of a "blue-eyed boy"? Were you overcome by a brown-eyed someone's warmth and affection? Or, conversely, was your dream subject a "green-eyed monster" of jealousy? Or perhaps you had a dream in which you found yourself gazing affectionately into the eyes of your wife. Can it be that your unconscious was reflecting your waking feeling that the two of you have been "seeing eye to eye" with one another, or was it expressing nostalgia for a time when you did?

Negative Interpretations: If you had a dream in which you were afflicted by a loss of vision or blindness, have you "closed your eyes" or "turned a blind eye" to some truth that you haven't wanted to "see" in the waking world? But if, in your dream, you found that putting on eyeglasses greatly improved your vision, then perhaps your unconscious was telling you that you need to examine or "focus on" some issue of importance in real life. Likewise, if your dreaming self was suffering from distorted vision or a squint, consider whether you have been looking at some issue in a skewed, or "cock-eyed," manner. Finally, if you had a dream in which you found yourself arguing with someone, and that someone told you to "Look me in the eye and tell me the truth," then have you been feeling guilty over a lie that you have recently told or a secret that you have been keeping?

Genitals

The most obvious and likely reference associated with the dream appearance of breasts and genitalia is sex. That said, sex is a large and complex subject—encompassing issues of intimacy, sexual orientation, and gender identity, virility, power, and so forth—and a dream that highlights genitals or breasts can have a number of other meanings, depending upon the specific context and your dreaming reaction.

Symbolic and Verbal Associations
› Sex and sexuality
› Virility; sexual potency
› Gender identity
› Mothering (when breastfeeding is highlighted)
› Castration; emasculation
› Impotence

Positive Interpretations: If you had a dream that homed in on genitalia, the most likely explanation is that it had to do with your real-life feelings about sex, intimacy, and/or—especially if you are a man—your anxiety about your sexual performance. The same can be said about the appearance of breasts in a dream, although—particularly if the dreamer is a woman, and if the dream involved breast-feeding—breasts can also symbolize one's hopes and fears with regard to childbearing and mothering. Of course, if your unconscious highlighted the genitals in a positive sexual way, it is most likely that you have experienced a wish-fulfillment dream. If you have a waking desire to undergo sex-change surgery, then wish fulfillment may also be the explanation of a dream in which you realized that you had developed the genitalia of the opposite sex. But if you have no such waking desire, then your unconscious mind may have been telling you that you need to balance your personality better by developing your masculine side (if you are a woman) or your feminine side (if you are a man), particularly with regard to your sex life (do you long to be more submissive or assertive in bed?).

Negative Interpretations: If you are a man who dreamed that your partner grew fangs and was about to bite off your penis, then you have experienced a classic male anxiety dream. The penis is a symbol of masculine power, and your dream may indicate that you are feeling impotent or emasculated because you perceive that your partner is the more dominant player in your relationship. (Dreams of impotence, which have to do with a loss of self-esteem, may also have a literal or real-life parallel.) On the other hand, if you are a woman who dreamed of castrating a man, then the meaning is the opposite: it is likely that you have waking feelings of resentment about this man's power over you, and that you long to render him impotent or less threatening or dominating in his behavior toward you.

Heads & Faces

Because the head houses the brain, its symbolism involves thinking, as well as the intellect, reasoning, and control (or the loss thereof). The head is also the location of the face, the part of us that we most often (and most prominently) present to the world. The face is a primary vehicle for determining how others will perceive us, and our dreams sometimes use the symbol of the face in order to direct our focus to our outer image or persona.

The Body

Symbolic and Verbal Associations

› The outer image or persona
› Thinking; reason; intelligence
› "Getting ahead"; progression
› "Losing face": humiliation
› Becoming "red-faced" or embarrassed
› Acting "big-headed" or "swollen-headed," (i.e., self-importantly)

Positive Interpretations: If you had a dream that focused on a head—no matter if it was your own head or someone else's—you should consider whether your dream was an unconscious reference to "getting ahead" (such as being promoted to the "head" of a board or committee), or else to reason or the intellect. When interpreting a dream in which, like the myth of Narcissus, you found yourself transfixed by the beauty of your own face, ask yourself if you wish that the world would recognize you for your good looks or for the attractiveness of your personality.

Negative Interpretations: If, in your dream, your boss delivered a painful blow to the side of your head, then is he or she putting too much pressure on you, and thereby giving you a "headache," in the real world? Or if you had a nightmare in which someone was about to cut off your head, who was that person? Is he or she aggravating or harassing you so much during waking hours that you feel that you are in danger of "losing your head" or acting rashly? Any dream in which your head swelled to a larger-than-life size could be an unconscious signal that you have become vain or "big-headed." If you were shocked to see that your dream face had frozen into a horrible grimace, could it be that you are worried that others may find you obnoxious or repulsive, perhaps because you have been consumed by an "ugly" emotion, such as jealousy or hatred? On the other hand, if you had a dream in which you were frightened by someone else's ugly face, this may be an unconscious warning that you will soon have to "face up" to something unpleasant. (Did you recognize the person in your dream? The unpleasantness to which your unconscious was referring may have something to do with that person.) Finally, if you dreamed that you looked into the mirror and saw that you had no face, do you feel that you have recently "lost face," or suffered a humiliation, in the real world?

Sickness

Unless you are really sick in the real world, or fear that you might be ill (in which case you should probably see a doctor in order to set your mind at ease), dream sickness rarely refers to physical health. Rather, sickness in a dream is usually a reference to our emotional wellbeing.

Symbolic and Verbal Associations
› Psychological or emotional wellbeing
› Emotional impairment
› Being in need of help or support
› A desire to be taken care of
› Being sickened or nauseated by something

The Body

Positive Interpretations: If you had a dream in which you were lying on sickbed, or in which you felt terribly ill (when, in reality, you are quite physically healthy), then this could have been an unconscious warning that you are not taking care of your body or mind—either because you are overworking yourself, because you are not eating properly, or because you have been drinking too much alcohol or using other substances—and that, if you do not alter your habits, you could end up making yourself very ill (either physically or emotionally, or both). Or if you basked in the attention of someone who was taking care of you, it is possible that you experienced a wish-fulfillment dream, or else that you are in need of some emotional support in the waking world.

Negative Interpretations: Your unconscious may use different medical conditions to symbolize specific emotional problems. For instance, if you dreamed that you were ill and in the hospital, and that your doctor told you that you were suffering from cancer, then is something "eating away" at you during your waking life? Could it be your guilt about the fact that you maybe haven't spoken to your mother in a year? In another scenario, if you dreamed that you were vomiting uncontrollably, is something in the real world making you feel sickened or nauseated? Or else, do you wish that you could purge yourself of a "sickening" problem or situation? If you dreamed that you couldn't breathe, is something causing you to gasp or "fight for breath" in the real world? Do you feel "suffocated" by your overneedy partner? If you had a dream in which you were paralyzed, numb, or felt nothing at all, then ask yourself whether you have become emotionally "numb" or unfeeling in the waking world. If you had a dream in which you were walking with crutches, do you feel that you are emotionally "crippled"? Or are you reliant upon chemical "crutches," such as alcohol or drugs? Finally, if you dreamed that you had contracted a contagious disease, do you feel that you have become a "social outcast" in the real world?

Teeth

We don't often think much about our teeth unless there is something wrong with one of them, and when teeth feature prominently in a dream, it is rarely in a positive light. Dreams of teeth often have to do with anxiety about something, and may be tied into our feelings about a recent loss or life change.

Symbolic and Verbal Associations

› Youth, vigour, or "bite"
› Losing our baby teeth; leaving childhood behind
› Ruminating on something, or "chewing it over"
› "Wisdom" teeth
› Anxiety about change or loss

Positive Interpretations: One of the primary functions of teeth is chewing, and when we are thinking about, or ruminating on, some issue or problem, we sometimes say that we are "chewing it over." So if you had a dream in which you were chewing and chewing on the same morsel of food, this may have been an unconscious allusion to some problem that you have been faced with in your waking hours; your dream may be a signal that you should "chew over" the facts a lot more before coming to a decision about how to address the problem. Or if you dreamed that your wisdom teeth (the hindmost molars) were emerging, have you actually been feeling wiser or more mature and responsible in the real world?

Negative Interpretations: Many people have experienced an anxiety dream about their teeth crumbling or falling out. Having a dream toothache could simply be due to the fact that you were grinding your teeth as you slumbered and your unconscious mind incorporated this into your dream. Some people grind their teeth while they sleep when they are under excessive stress during waking hours, and if you awoke to find that your jaws were clenched and sore, you should probably see your dentist to discuss whether this could be the case for you. Dreams about tooth pain or loss could also signify that you are feeling anxious about a significant life change. Have you recently quit your job, or are you and your spouse discussing divorce? Or if you dreamed that your teeth fell out, have you recently lost a loved one? Are you about to move to another part of the country, leaving your friends and family behind? Or could it be that you are anxious about growing older and losing your vigor or your "bite"? Anxiety (whether about visiting the dentist or about a forthcoming event) is also the likely meaning if you had a dream in which a dentist shone a bright light in your face as he or she poked and prodded inside your mouth. The other major function of teeth is biting, and if you dreamed that someone you know threatened to bite (or actually bit) you, could it be that this person really harbors some anger or hostility toward you?

The Life Cycle

Dreams of being younger or older than you actually are may have been triggered by all manner of latent emotions, such as feelings of nostalgia or worries about aging and a desire to turn back your body clock. Dreams like these may alternatively symbolically portray your conscious or unconscious state of mind, and especially your desires and dreads. That said, sometimes they merely echo your conscious preoccupations with aspects of your real-world situation.

Adolescence

Adolescence is a very special time of transition in life as it is the segue from childhood to adulthood. In dreams, the appearance of teenagers often has to do with youthful attitudes and behavior, as well as with those issues that people generally must face during adolescence.

Symbolic and Verbal Associations
> Youthful attitudes and behavior
> Rebellion
> Enthusiasm and ambition
> Stubbornness; willfulness
> A carefree attitude

Positive Interpretations: If you had a dream that focused on a teenager, particularly if this teenager was unknown to you and if you found yourself reacting to him or her with admiration, then this may have been your unconscious mind's way of urging you to adopt a more youthful outlook on life. If you are a man who dreamed of an adolescent boy, what about him did you admire? Was it his carefree abandon? His rebellious idealism? His energy and vitality? Or if you are a woman who dreamed of a teenaged girl, what struck you about her? Was it her enthusiasm for life? Her sense of wonder at the world? Her positive outlook? Whatever the quality, it may be that this aspect of your own self has become atrophied or faded over the years—and if you worked to redevelop it, then you may find that you would be much happier, with a restored joy of living. On the other hand, if you are a woman who dreamed of a teenaged boy, or if you are a man who dreamed of a teenaged girl, then you should consider whether you may have been visited by your animus (if you are a woman) or your anima (if you are a man)—a character whose appearance in your dream may indicate the need for your waking self to develop a better internal gender balance.

Negative Interpretations: If you dreamed of being a teenager again, could it be that you are in mourning over the loss (or the perceived loss) of your youthful looks, vitality, and/or outlook on life? Or could it be that you regret that you did not "make the most" of your youthful potential at a time when (you now realize, with hindsight) "the world was at your feet"? If you had a dream in which you were upset by a teenager's rudeness, willfulness, or bad behavior, then this may have been your unconscious mind's attempt to push you to recognize such behavior in your waking self. For instance, have you been rebelling against the advice of an authority figure (such as a professor or a boss) because you do not want to recognize that you are wrong about some issue? Or if you had a dream in which a teenager hurt your feelings by ridiculing you, what was it that he or she said that most wounded you? Was it your stodgy unwillingness to open your mind to new ideas? If so, then could he or she have been right?

Birth

When the unconscious mind summons the theme of birth into our dreams, the meaning often has less to do with a real-life baby than with a metaphorical one. Dreams of this nature may be a reference to the "inner child," or the "baby" within, or even to a part of yourself that longs to be reborn.

Symbolic and Verbal Associations

› The "inner child"
› Rebirth or a reawakening of some part of oneself; new potential
› Hopes and fears with regard to an actual pregnancy
› Laboring to give birth to an idea; a "brainchild"

Positive Interpretations: If you are a pregnant woman who dreamed of giving birth to your baby, then it is likely that your dream was a reflection of your hopes and fears with regard to your impending due date. (A similar interpretation will apply if you are a prospective father who dreamed of your partner giving birth.) If the dream labor and birthing were easy, then your unconscious was probably attempting to set your mind at ease with this wish-fulfillment dream. However, if you are a woman who dreamed of giving birth and if you are not actually pregnant in the real world, then it is possible that your dream was pointing to your desire to have a child. On the other hand, whether you are a man or a woman, a dream of giving birth may also be a reference to a "brainchild"—an idea, plan, or project that you have been thinking about during waking hours. Did the labor go smoothly? And were you ecstatic because you had given birth to a healthy newborn? If so, your unconscious mind was probably trying to reassure you that your plans will pan out well. Did your dream self give birth to twins? If so, your dream may have been a reference to "twin" ideas or aspects of yourself, such as your writing and musical talents.

Negative Interpretations: Did you dream of undergoing a difficult and painful labor? If so, and if you are actually pregnant, then your dream was probably mirroring your anxieties—perhaps in an effort to force you to face up to your fears, thereby strengthening you and preparing you for the upcoming day or night when you actually will go into labor. In your dream, were you surprised to see that you'd given birth to an animal, or even to a monster? Again, this sort of dream is likely to be a reference to your real-life worries. Or a dream of a difficult labor may be a reference to an idea or a "brainchild." Was the umbilical cord wrapped around your brainchild's neck? If so, then your unconscious may have been indicating that your idea is in danger of being "strangled at birth." Or if you labored in vain, unable to give birth to your baby, it is possible that your unconscious was trying to tell you that your waking plans or ideas will be difficult—if not impossible—to carry out at this time. The same interpretation may apply if, in your dream, you were aggrieved to have given birth to an unhealthy or a stillborn child.

Childhood

A dream youngster is often a symbol of the "inner child"—the aspect of oneself that is carefree, playful, and innocent. Childhood is also a time when we learn many of the lessons that we will keep with us and reference later in life, so that a dream in which you revisited some scenario from your childhood may have been an unconscious reminder of an important lesson that may have some relevance to your current situation.

Symbolic and Verbal Associations
› The "inner child"
› Fun; play
› Having a simple perspective on life
› Innocence and wonder
› Lessons learned

Positive Interpretations: Did a dream take you back to a pleasant memory from your childhood? Perhaps you were sitting contentedly on your father's lap while he read to you from your favorite book? There are two likely explanations for a dream of this sort. The first explanation is that your dream was an unconscious manifestation of your nostalgia for a simpler time, when life was filled with fun and you had no responsibilities and few worries. (The second explanation will be discussed below, in Negative Interpretations.) If your dream called up a child who you did not know, then your unconscious mind may have been summoning the archetype of the "inner child"—either as a representation of the part of you that never grew up, or as a reference to a part of you that you have lost (but that you would do well to regain).

Negative Interpretations: The other explanation for a nostalgic childhood dream is that, by reminding you of how happy and secure you felt as a small child, your unconscious mind was attempting to comfort you and to compensate for your adult unhappiness. If you are facing a difficult problem or situation in the real world, then it is also possible that your dream called upon the image of your father because he was someone who always gave you good advice; your unconscious mind may have been hinting that you would do well to remember the lessons that he taught you, or it may have been prompting you to seek out someone who would be likely to give you wise counsel in your present life. Alternatively, did you dream of a child who upset you with his or her bad or immature behavior? If so, could this have been a dream reference to your own childish bad conduct in the waking world? For instance, did you dream that you were watching a group of children playing, and that you were appalled when a bigger boy went up to a smaller girl and pushed her down into the dirt? If so, have you been playing the bully with someone less powerful than you—perhaps a junior colleague onto whom you've been dumping your workload?

Coming of Age

In our culture today, there seems to be no consensus on when we enter adulthood. This is no wonder, when we are given adult freedoms in such small increments; for instance, we can get a driver's license at age sixteen, join the military at age eighteen, purchase alcohol at age twenty-one, and rent a car at age twenty-five! Each of these milestones will have varying degrees of personal significance for different people, however, and each of them (as well as many more, such as going to college, getting married, and achieving financial independence) are moments in which we step farther into the world of adults.

Symbolic and Verbal Associations

› Freedom
› Taking on adult responsibilities and making adult decisions
› Having to "stand on your own two feet"
› "Flying the nest," or leaving one's parents' home
› The "empty nest"

Positive Interpretations: Did you have a dream in which you relived some moment from your past that you felt represented the end of your childhood and that ushered you into your adult life? Perhaps it was the first time that you stood up to your father, or the day you moved into your first apartment? If so, and if you awoke from this dream with a thrilling rush of adrenaline, then it is likely that your unconscious mind summoned up this memory in order to remind you that it is once again time to take the initiative and to "stand on your own two feet" in the world. If you've been feeling somehow "smothered" or "kept down" in the real world—perhaps by an over-dominant partner or parent—then your unconscious may have been trying to remind you how positive and good it felt to "break loose" on your own.

Negative Interpretations: Did you dream that you stood weeping as your son read from the Torah at his bar mitzvah (the ceremony in which Jewish boys, at the age of thirteen, are initiated into adulthood)? And, in reality, did your son have his bar mitzvah years ago? If so, is he about to take another big life step, such as going away to college, joining the army, or getting married? If so, then your dream was probably a reflection of your sadness and fears with regard to "losing" your son; perhaps you feel as though your home will be an "empty nest" once he is "gone" from you. Or, did you dream that your daughter (who, in reality, is now happily married, with children of her own) was once again in her first term at college and rebelling against your authority by staying out at all hours and using illegal drugs or alcohol? If so, then could it be that you feel as though your daughter no longer consults you or wants to be "mothered" by you in the waking world? Or, as when she was in college, is she once again engaging in some activity that you feel is dangerous or destructive?

Conception

Conception has been a high-profile media topic for some time now, as many people who oppose the right to abortion maintain that life begins at the moment that we are conceived, while their opponents often argue that life truly begins at a later stage of fetal development, or even at birth. Everyone must agree, however, that conception is at least the dawn of the creation of a new potential life, and dreams that involve conception may be literal (especially if becoming pregnant has been on your mind) or they may be metaphors for creation of another type.

Symbolic and Verbal Associations
› Sexual union; the merging of male and female
› New beginnings; fresh potential
› Creation and creativity; the "fertilization" of a concept
› Apprehension about or fear of becoming pregnant

Positive Interpretations: If you are a woman, did you awake from a sexual dream in which you were certain that you had just conceived a baby? And were you over-joyed by that knowledge? If so, and if you are hoping to become pregnant in the real world, then you have probably experienced a wish-fulfillment dream (although it is also possible that your unconscious mind has detected that you are, in fact, pregnant, and that it sent you this dream in an attempt to bring this fact to your conscious attention). If you are a man who dreamed that your partner had conceived, which made your dream self very happy, then, likewise, your unconscious mind was probably giving expression to your fervent wish to have a child. However, there is another line of interpretation for dreams of this type. If you dreamed that you (or your partner) had conceived, and if nothing is farther from your mind, then your dream conception may have been a reference to the fertilization of a creative concept. Have you recently hit upon a good idea in the waking world?

Negative Interpretations: If you are a woman who had a dream in which you were apprehensive or uneasy because you thought that you had conceived a baby, then have you been debating whether to try to become pregnant in the waking world? If so, then your dream may have been a reflection of your real-life uncertainty as to whether having a child would be a good idea at this time. (Perhaps you feel you are not ready to expand your family, but have been feeling pressured to do so by your partner or your relatives.) If you were horror-struck by your dream conception, then it is likely that your dream was expressing your waking fears that you have accidentally conceived (or could accidentally conceive) a child—and your unconscious may have been attempting to jolt you into taking more sound precautions against pregnancy. Similar interpretations will apply if you are a man who reacted ambivalently or negatively to a dream that your partner had conceived.

Death

Although everyone knows that they and their loved ones must one day die, not many people like to think about this fact, and, for most people, dreams that involve death are among the most disturbing. When our unconscious mind forces us to experience dreams about death, however, there are many possible interpretations, and not all of them have to do with the actual ending of someone's life.

Symbolic and Verbal Associations

› Loss
› Endings (and beginnings); the end of a relationship
› Life changes
› Loneliness

Positive Interpretations: Did you awake in tears from a dream in which you watched as your grandmother died? If so, and if your grandmother's health is failing in the real world, then your dream probably reflected your sadness at the thought of losing her, and it may also have been your unconscious's way of preparing you for her inevitable demise. If, in your dream, you felt greatly relieved at your grandmother's passing, then it may be that you have already come to terms with her approaching death, which you know will release her from her suffering. But if you dreamed of the death of a loved one who is quite well in the real world, then it could be that this person represented some part of yourself or your life that either is passing away or that you would like to be done with. Unless your own death is near (if you suffer from a fatal disease, for instance), then a dream that highlights your own death is highly unlikely to portend your actual demise. There are three possible explanations for a dream such as this: first, that you are concerned about your health (in which case, a visit to the doctor may be in order); second, that you seek an "escape" from something in your world; or, third, that your dream death signaled a life change that you are about to make (which is a sort of metaphorical death, but also a new beginning).

Negative Interpretations: A dream involving the death of a loved one may also reflect our own feelings of guilt about having neglected our responsibilities to that person or about our failure to tell them how much they mean to us. This type of interpretation may apply if, for instance, you dreamed that your sister had died, and if you were deeply saddened—not just by her passing, but also because you had not had a last chance to tell her that you love her. Another interpretation is that you feel as though your sister has been drifting away from you, and you feel that your relationship with her is in danger of ending altogether (in which case, your unconscious may have been trying to prompt you to mend the rift between your sister and yourself). Alternatively, if you felt relieved or liberated by your sister's dream death, this may reflect your unconscious desire to end your relationship with her, perhaps because you feel it has become unhealthy for you.

Miscarriages

If you dreamed that you had a miscarriage, an abortion, or a stillbirth, you probably awoke feeling saddened and disturbed (at the very least). All of these things have to do with expulsions – of something (or someone significant) from ourselves. The various dream-world meanings may involve anxiety or guilt.

Symbolic and Verbal Associations
› Anxiety (possibly—but not necessarily—about pregnancy)
› A concept or idea that is doomed to failure
› The desire to abort (or rid oneself of) something
› Feelings of guilt
› A "miscarriage" of duty or justice

Positive Interpretations: A dream of having a miscarriage, an abortion, or a stillbirth (particularly if you are actually pregnant) probably left you feeling deeply upset when you awoke. However, if you are really pregnant, while it is always a possibility that your nightmare was a message from your unconscious mind that your unborn child is not developing properly, the far more likely scenario is that your unconscious was reflecting your normal feelings of anxiety with regard to your pregnancy. Alternatively, could your dream abortion or miscarriage have been an unconscious clue that you are not ready to make some great personal sacrifice, such as becoming a mother (and therefore assuming complete responsibility for another human being) would require?

Negative Interpretations: If you are someone who is not, and perhaps cannot be, pregnant, the vast majority of dream miscarriages, abortions, or stillbirths will refer to an idea or concept that you have "conceived," which your unconscious mind may be telling you is doomed to fail. How did your dream self react? Was the termination of your dream pregnancy against your will? If so, was someone else responsible? And could you identify that person? It is possible that your unconscious mind cast him or her in the role of your abortionist in order to signal that he or she is set on thwarting some plan of yours in the real world. (Perhaps it was your neighbor, who has been secretly hacking away at your rose bushes because he is jealous that they might grower higher than his own.) However, if your dream self wanted the abortion, or was glad for your miscarriage, then it is possible that (for whatever reason) your unconscious mind was warning you against the current plan or idea that has been developing in your mind. Or could your dream of having an abortion have been a metaphor for something that you feel guilty about in the waking world? (If so, your unconscious may have been prompting you to "kill off" or to "get rid of" the evidence of whatever has been causing you distress.)

Old Age

When our unconscious mind places an older person at the forefront of our dreams, it may do so in order to highlight those positive qualities that we associate with old age: experience, wisdom, and kindness. But, like most dream symbols, old age also has a flip or dark side, having to do with cruelty and the selfish use of power.

Symbolic and Verbal Associations

› Wisdom and guidance
› The archetype of the priest or the priestess
› The archetypal witch or the black magician
› Anxiety with regard to growing older
› Mortality: decline and death

Positive Interpretations: If your dream cast a spotlight on an older man or woman, did you know who he or she was? If it was one of your grandparents, for instance, then his or her appearance in your dream may have filled you with a feeling of happy nostalgia, perhaps reminding you of how simple and good life could be when you were a child. And because we tend to associate growing older with achieving a certain amount of wisdom, you may want to consider whether the older person whom you dreamed of could have represented an archetype—perhaps the priestess (the wise old woman) or the priest (the wise old man)—thereby indicating that you are in need of some guidance in the waking world. (In your dream, what did the older person say to you?) Or if your dream image was one of yourself, well-aged and contented, perhaps sitting on your front porch and bouncing your young grandchild on your knee, then have you been feeling stressed and frazzled in your waking hours? Do you wish that you could retire from your job and enjoy the rest of your days in peace? Your unconscious may have sent you this dream in order to give you a taste of the release that you seek.

Negative Interpretations: Did you dream of an older person who, by their wickedness, filled you with dread? The negative aspects of the priestess and the priest are the archetypes of the witch and the black magician. Though equally knowledgeable and powerful, these characters use their knowledge and power destructively, to advance their own dark agendas. Did you recognize the evil elder in your dream? Your unconscious may have been warning you that you should scrutinize the motives of this person, who may be intending to do you ill. Or could the witch's or the black magician's appearance in your dream have been a signal that your own dark side has begun to gain power over you? Alternatively, if you had a dream in which you were horrified to discover that you had rapidly advanced in years, so that you had become, all of a sudden, an old man or woman, then it is likely that your unconscious was expressing your fears or regrets about the inevitability of growing older and—ultimately—your own mortality.

Parenthood

The parent–child relationship is one of the strongest and most fundamentally important relationships that exist, and, therefore, the concept of parenting lends a generous load of fodder to the symbolic world of dreams.

Symbolic and Verbal Associations

› Care-giving (both physical and emotional)
› Providing guidance to (and exerting authority over) someone
› The "child within"
› Your hopes or fears with regard to a symbolic "child" (a plan or idea, perhaps)
› Frustration with demands that others make upon us; lack of personal time

Positive Interpretations: Did you dream that you were the proud parent of a healthy, happy son or daughter? If you do not have any children in the real world—and if, in fact, having children is something you're not even considering—then it is likely that your dream was a reference to a symbolic "child". It could refer to a plan or idea of yours that has begun to grow and prosper in the real world. If the child was excessively demanding of your attention, then your unconscious may have been indicating that your "brainchild" will require a lot of nurturing from you in order for it to thrive. Alternatively, did you find your dream self "parenting" someone whom you know in the real world—maybe a friend or a coworker? If so, then you may want to ask yourself whether you have been feeling protective of, or responsible for, this person, or if this person somehow needs your help or guidance. (And your dream self's reaction is likely to be an indication of the health of your relationship with him or her in the waking world.)

Negative Interpretations: If you had a dream in which you were the parent of a child who screamed constantly, so that your peace of mind was wrecked to bits, then your unconscious mind may have been indicating that you have been neglecting or failing to care for your new idea or project properly (perhaps you have taken on more responsibility than you are currently capable of handling). Or if you had a nightmare in which you lost, injured, or otherwise allowed some harm to come to your dream child, then do you fear that your self-perceived flaws or inadequacies will cause a similar fate to befall the results of your hard work in the real world? Or perhaps it could have indicated that something you're trying to plan is simply not meant to be. However, if your dream child corresponded with someone from your waking world (perhaps your actual child), then it is likely that your dream was mirroring your current mental state. Have you been feeling overburdened (and guilt-ridden) by the demands of others (perhaps your real-life children), so that you find that you are unable to cope with everyday life?

Relationships

Because we see or communicate with some people regularly, and perhaps even daily, or they remain present in our thoughts even if physically absent, it is hardly surprising that our dreams are typically populated by the people with whom we interact most in the real world. And when they materialize in dreamland, they may either represent themselves and the type of relationship that we actually have—or else hope or fear having—with them, or they may symbolize a certain characteristic within ourselves.

Children

Because the parent–child relationship is usually very strong, and because most parents are deeply in tune with what is happening with their children, the meaning of a dream that involves one's own child is often very clear-cut and easy to deduce.

Symbolic and Verbal Associations
› Maternal or paternal feelings
› Ideological progeny: a "brainchild"
› A masculine or feminine archetype
› Childlike attitudes or behavior

Positive Interpretations: If you are a parent who had a dream that involved your child, then the meaning of your dream is probably a straightforward one. For instance, if you dreamed that you were filled with pride and love as you watched your daughter perform the lead role in a school play, then it is likely that your dream was an expression of the pride and love that you feel for your daughter in the real world. On the other hand, if you had a dream such as this, but, in reality, you do not have any children, then it is possible that you experienced a wish-fulfillment dream. It is also possible that your dream child represented a "brainchild"—an idea, plan, or project that you have given (or are about to give) life to. However, if none of these explanations seems likely, then you should ask yourself whether your dream child could have represented one of the many masculine or feminine archetypes—especially the princess (the unspoiled heroine), the prince (who represents the idealistic and questing nature of youth), the amazon (who represents the intellect and practicality), the warrior (the archetypical hero), or the trickster (an attention-seeker who uses jests and tricks to sabotage the status quo—often for good reason).

Negative Interpretations: Again, because a dream that involves one's own child can usually be taken at face value, if you are a parent who dreamed that your daughter was in danger or that she had been injured, then you are probably worried about her safety in the real world. (Has she recently taken up a sport or hobby that involves physical risk, such as skateboarding?) Or did you have a dream in which your son railed against you for not understanding where he is "coming from" or for not taking his opinions seriously? If so, it is likely that your unconscious mind was trying to alert you to the fact that, in reality, you haven't been listening to, or giving enough attention to, your son, and that you would do well to prioritize spending some "quality" time with him. However, especially if you do not have children of your own, you should consider whether your dream child may have represented one of the dark or more sinister archetypes, including the siren (or selfish seductress), the wastrel (the irresponsible philanderer), the huntress (who hunts down and uses others for her own purposes), or the villain (who uses cunning or violence for evil ends).

Enemies

If you awoke from a dream that centered on your arch enemy or rival, this was probably an unpleasant experience (to say the least)—unless, of course, your dreaming mind transformed your worst foe into a trusting friend, in which case you are probably more perplexed than upset. But what do dreams of this nature mean?

Symbolic and Verbal Associations

› Conflict or hostility; a challenge
› A warning of an attack (not necessarily physical); the need to stay "on your toes"
› Atonement, or a desire to make peace with someone
› An internal conflict; "the enemy within"

Positive Interpretations: Were you surprised by a dream in which you quarreled and then made up with your worst enemy? Did your dream end with the two of you having drinks together and laughing over your old feud? If so, your dream may be an unconscious indication that the two of you may be able to "bury the hatchet," or come to a settlement over whatever it is that has divided you in the real world. Or if, in your dream, you were making a sincere apology to your enemy, and were pleading with him or her to forgive you for something that you have done, could it be that you are feeling guilty over the way that you have treated this person in the waking world? Your unconscious may have been telling you that you should take responsibility and make amends for your role in the conflict that you have had with this person.

Negative Interpretations: If you dreamed that you had a heated argument or fight with your most hated enemy, the most likely explanation is that your unconscious was merely mirroring your waking-life dislike of that person, his or her antipathy toward you, or your mutual abhorrence of each other. And if, in your dream, it was you who instigated and dominated the conflict, then your dream may have served as a safety valve, providing you with an outlet for the pent-up anger and aggression that you feel toward this person. Alternatively, if you had a dream that you were under some sort of attack (be it physical or psychological) by your enemy, your unconscious mind may have been warning you that this person has been plotting against you, and that you are in danger of a similar attack in the real world. Finally, if your dreaming mind conjured up an enemy whom you did not recognize, then you may want to consider whether you are in conflict with some aspect of yourself, or "the enemy within". What did your dream enemy look like? And can you remember what it was that you were arguing or fighting over? (For instance, if you are a somewhat conservative man and you dreamed that you argued with a teenager over politics, then the teenager may have represented a more youthful and adventurous part of yourself that longs to be expressed in the waking world.)

Ex-lovers & Ex-spouses

Though a few people manage to cultivate good, healthy friendships with their exes, most people tend not to have very positive feelings toward their ex-lovers and ex-spouses. And if you had a dream in which you were visited by an ex, you were probably left wondering why your unconscious mind chose to put you through such grief.

Symbolic and Verbal Associations

› Jealousy
› Guilt
› Anger; rage; hostility
› Insecurity
› Deceit

Positive Interpretations: Were you perplexed by a dream that took you back to a scene from a less-than-happy old relationship, and are you in a positive, loving relationship now? Perhaps you dreamed of your ex-husband coming home in the middle of the night, when you knew that he had been cheating on you with another woman. Your unconscious mind's reason for forcing you to relive such a scenario may have been simply to remind you of how lucky and happy you are to have your current husband or boyfriend. Alternatively, did you dream of happy times with an ex? If so, there are a few possible explanations. It is possible that your unconscious mind was reminding you of the inherent goodness that lies inside your ex-partner, perhaps so that you might find the courage to "bury the hatchet" and become friends with (or, at least, let go of your anger for) this person. Of course, it is also possible that your dream is an indication that you still have romantic feelings for your ex, and only you will know if this is the case.

Negative Interpretations: Did your ex-wife make an appearance in your dream, and did she "push your buttons" in the same way that she did before you were divorced? If so, and if she is still a part of your life in some way (perhaps you have to see each other because you share custody of a child), then your dream was probably just a reflection of your real-life feelings for your ex-wife. It is also possible that you are worried about a threat that you perceive that she may be posing to you. (For instance, has she been threatening to seek full custody of your child, or do you feel that she has been "poisoning" your child's mind against you?) Or did you have a dream in which you knocked your cocky ex-husband on the head with his favorite golf club? If so, you probably experienced a safety-valve dream—i.e., your unconscious mind was allowing you to act out the rage that you feel toward your ex in the safety of dreamland. However, it is also possible that your dream was a warning that your feelings of anger are overtaking you and that you are in danger of losing control and actually committing some violent act toward your ex.

Fathers

For many people, their father is one of the most dominant, significant influences in their lives. (And even if you grew up without a father, his absence was likely to have exerted a considerable force and influence on your psyche.) When interpreting a dream that centered on your father, you should take into consideration what sort of relationship you have (or had) with him (if any at all)—particularly when you were a child—as well as how this makes you feel.

Symbolic and Verbal Associations

› Love and caring
› Dependence on someone
› Authority and discipline
› Respect
› Benevolence
› The ogre (or the negative, power-hungry father)

Positive Interpretations: If you had a dream in which your gentle and loving father put his arm around you and told you how proud of you he was, then your dream was probably underlining the important, positive role that your father has played in your life (though your dream may also indicate that you have been feeling somewhat insecure lately and that you could use some loving reassurance). Or were you surprised by a dream in which your father, who, in real life, was always overly aggressive and hurtful, acted in a way that was compassionate and loving? In this case, your unconscious mind may have invoked the archetype of the ideal male parent, possibly because you are in need of this type of father figure in your current life, or possibly to tell you that it's time for you to fulfill this role for your own self (or even for someone else in your life).

Negative Interpretations: Did you dream that your father gave you a stern lecture about your spending habits? If so, and if you have memories of him chiding you for wasting your money when you were a teenager, then your dream was probably pointing to your own judgment against yourself because you feel that you are not living up to the standards that your father set for you. However, if your father was always gentle and loving, and if you had a dream in which he behaved aggressively or cruelly toward you, then your unconscious may have conjured up the archetype of the power-hungry ogre—perhaps to alert you to someone who is behaving like an "ogre" in your current life. (For instance, could the dream ogre have represented your over-controlling boss, who has been bullying and demeaning you at work?) Finally, if you have recurring negative dreams about your father, this may be an indication that you need to become more independent of him (or of his memory), and that it's time for you to live your life according to your own rules and values.

Friends

Our closest friends are a source of companionship and emotional support, and we depend on them for many things. Most people will have a number of similarities with their friends, in term of personality and interests, as well as differences, and a dream that involves a friend may highlight an aspect of that friend's character or personality or of our relationship with him or her (sometimes in order to tell us something about ourselves, as the unconscious will often project aspects of ourselves onto those who are closest to us).

Symbolic and Verbal Associations

› Camaraderie
› Trust
› A reunion
› Emotional dependence
› An aspect of your own character

Positive Interpretations: Did you have a dream in which you and your closest friend participated in an activity that the two of you always do together? Perhaps you dreamed that you and your friend were chatting and listening to music as you shared a pot of tea at her house—something that you do at least two times a week. If so, then your unconscious was probably mirroring your real-life relationship with your best friend, and the important role that she plays in your life. The same interpretation will apply if you and your best friend no longer live close to each other, and face-to-face interactions have become infrequent—although, in this case, your dream was probably a signal that you miss your friend and that it may be time for a visit.

Negative Interpretations: Did you dream that you looked on with terror and dismay as your best friend, who has a bit of a hot temper, started a fist fight with a group of people at a bar, so that he was handcuffed and arrested by the police? When the unconscious highlights or exaggerates a characteristic or the behavior of one of your friends, it may do so for one of two reasons. On the one hand, your dream may have been a sign that, although you make light of, and are often amused by, your friend's temper, his tendency to "blow up" is making you feel uneasy or afraid. On the other hand, however, your dream may have been a warning that it is you, and not your friend, who is in danger of letting your temper lead you into real trouble. Alternatively, in your dream, did your friend turn his violent temper against you? If so, you probably awoke feeling extremely troubled, and perhaps angry with your friend. This type of dream may indicate that there is some underlying trouble in your relationship with your friend—perhaps something that neither of you is consciously aware of—and examining the details of the dream and your friend's behavior (both in the dream world and in real life) will provide clues.

Lovers

A fixation on love and sex—or on seeking or wooing a lover—is a major preoccupation in the lives of many, many people. The desire for love and sex is basic to human nature, and it is not surprising that dreams of these themes are quite common.

Symbolic and Verbal Associations

› Love and affection
› Romance
› Sexual desire
› Partnership
› Commitment

Positive Interpretations: Did you have a dream in which you felt the vibrant euphoria of sharing a passionate moment with your current lover, whom you are desperately in love with? If so, your dream may have been simply reaffirming your waking feelings of love for him or her. Or if things have begun to settle into a routine with your lover, so that the feelings of romance and desire are no longer as strong as they used to be, then your dream may have been a reminder from your unconscious of how you used to feel toward your lover (and may continue to feel, although you may not be as conscious of your feelings as you were before). If this is the case, then your unconscious may have been prompting you to make a conscious effort to rekindle the romance between yourself and your lover. Alternatively, if you experienced this sort of romantic dream and if you have no lover in the real world, then your dream was probably reflecting your desire to be in a relationship. (And did you know your dream lover? What qualities did he or she possess that attracted you?)

Negative Interpretations: Were you upset by a dream in which you and your lover were engaged in a vicious argument? If so, can you remember what you were arguing about? Your unconscious mind may have been highlighting a problem that has, thus far, gone under the radar of your conscious mind. Alternatively, were you taken aback or unsettled by a dream in which you were in love with someone whom you regard as playing a relatively minor role in your life (such as a coworker, or the cashier at your supermarket)? (Perhaps, even, you are actually attracted to this person in real life, but you have been fighting your feelings because you feel that they are not appropriate.) If so, you were probably extremely troubled by your dream—especially if either you or the person you dreamed of are in another relationship. However, as difficult as it may be to admit, your unconscious mind probably sent you this dream in order to provide an outlet for the romantic feelings that you have suppressed in the waking world. And it is also possible that your dream was encouraging you to express your feelings for this person in the real world.

Mothers

Perhaps no bond is stronger than the mother–child relationship when it is in its ideal form (i.e., gentle, loving, and nurturing). For a significant part of your life, you were probably emotionally and physically dependent on your mother (or—if she was absent from your life—on an alternative mother figure). And how you react to a dream that involved your mother will be tied into your feelings for her in the real world.

Symbolic and Verbal Associations
› Selflessness
› Tenderness and affection
› Nurturing
› The desire to "mother" (or to be "mothered" by) someone
› The archetype of the "terrible mother"

Positive Interpretations: Did you dream that your mother (who was always affectionate, tender, and loving toward you in the real world) held you in her arms, kissed you, and told you how much she loved you? If so, your dream was most likely mirroring your mother's importance in your life. It is also possible that your dream was an indication that you are currently in need of some "mothering" (perhaps because you have been feeling sad, lonely, or insecure). On the other hand, did you dream that your emotionally withdrawn, perhaps even spiteful or vindictive, mother had become full of love and compassion? If so, you probably awoke feeling a bit confused. The most likely explanation for this sort of dream is that your unconscious mind may have conjured up the archetype of the ideal mother (such as the Virgin Mary of Christianity), who represents selfless nurturing and unconditional love—perhaps indicating that you are in need of a "mothering" influence in your life (even if it is your own self who must mother you), or perhaps indicating that you are being called to "mother" someone else.

Negative Interpretations: Did you have a dream in which your overly critical mother was in prime form, berating you because of her disapproval of your hair-style or clothing? If so, then your dream may have been an unconscious form of self-admonishment, signifying that you are feeling badly about yourself because you feel that you are not living up to the standards that your mother instilled in you. However, if you dreamed such a dream and, in reality, your mother has never had an unkind word to say to you, then it may be that your dream self was visited by the archetype of the "terrible mother," the mother's dark side, who is cruel, dominating, critical, and under-mining. If so, you should ask yourself whether some-one in your current life has had a damaging effect on you by being overly controlling or selfish. Finally, if you have recurring negative dreams about your mother, you may want to consider whether you are too focused on her values and expectations of you; it may be time to set off on your own course in life.

Siblings

Because our brothers and sisters are usually around the same age as us, our relationships with them are prob-ably less encumbered by the quest for independence that so often causes difficulties in our interactions with our mother and father. However, this is not to say that our relationships with our siblings are simpler or less troubled: in fact, the conflicts that arise out of sibling rivalry tend to surface frequently in most people's conscious—and unconscious—minds.

Symbolic and Verbal Associations

› Sibling rivalry
› Platonic love
› Jealousy
› Bullying
› One's own self

Positive Interpretations: If you had a dream that mirrored the real-world, positive, and loving relationship that you have with your brother or sister, then your dream can almost certainly be taken at face value. However, if you are an only child and you dreamed of having a brother or sister, or if you dreamed that your real-life brother or sister behaved completely out of character, then it is quite likely that your dream had absolutely nothing to do with your family. Instead, your unconscious mind may have called up the image of a sibling in order to place the spotlight on some characteristic or aspect of your own self. For instance, if your normally angry and rude sister behaved courteously and lovingly in your dream, then your unconscious may have used the image of your sister in order to "set an example" for you to follow in your daily life. In another scenario, if your dream cast someone unrelated to you in the role of your sibling, this usually means that you have brotherly or sisterly feelings for him or her—along with all of the undercurrents of rivalry and platonic love that come with a sibling relationship.

Negative Interpretations: If you had a dream in which your brother or sister behaved in a way that angered or disturbed you—especially if their dream behaviour was typical of the way that he or she behaves (or the way that he or she used to behave) in the real world—then your dream was likely to have been a reflection of your unresolved childhood issues with regard to that sibling. So if your brother teased and bullied you in your dream in the same way that he did when you were children (and in the same way that he may continue to do today), then your unconscious may have been prompting you to take action and confront your brother about his behaviour. However, as discussed above under "Positive Interpretations," it is also possible that your dream sibling's bad behaviour was really a reflection of your own self—and thinking about your sibling's real-life behaviour, as well as your own, should help you decide if this is the case.

Spouses

Marriage has many abstract, yet powerful, associations, including love, commitment, and partnership. And in the world of dreams, when the unconscious calls up the image of a wife or a husband (whether or not they represent an actual person in the real world), it is to these primary associations that we should first look when we are trying to make sense of our dream.

Symbolic and Verbal Associations

› Love and commitment
› Contentment and security
› Anxiety about the stability of one's domestic life
› Partnership
› A masculine or feminine archetype

Positive Interpretations: If you had a dream in which you found yourself sharing a happy, loving moment with your husband or wife, the meaning of your dream will depend, in part, on your current life situation. So if your real-world partnership with your spouse is as loving and warm as it was in your dream, then your dream was surely reflecting and affirming this reality. However, if your marriage has been plagued by difficulties or quarrelling, then it is likely that your unconscious sent you the dream in order to remind you of the love that you feel for your partner, and perhaps to encourage you to not give up hope of regaining a functional, caring relationship with him or her. On the other hand, what if you experienced such a dream but, in reality, you are unmarried? If it is your deepest desire to find someone to share your life with, then you may have experienced a wish-fulfilment dream. But if you have no plan or desire to become wedded, then you may want to consider whether your dream spouse could have been a female or male archetype—possibly even your anima or animus, the alter ego of your soul.

Negative Interpretations: Did you have a nightmare in which your worst fears regarding your husband or wife were played out upon the stage of your mind? Perhaps you woke up feeling like your heart was in your throat because you'd dreamed that you caught your wife of twenty years engaged in a sex act with another man. If so, your dream was probably just an expression of your insecurity or worries about your wife's faithfulness and dedication to you—although the dream may also have been an indication that you have unconsciously (or even consciously) perceived that your wife may, in fact, be cheating on you, in which case your unconscious mind may have been trying to prepare you to confront and deal with this reality. Lastly, if you dreamed of arguing or fighting with your spouse, then your unconscious may have been pointing to some issue or problem in your relationship—and if you can remember what it was that you were quarrelling over, then this may give you a clue to the real-life issue.

Archetypal & Symbolic Figures

According to Jung, the archetypes are symbolic representations of human emotions, traits, and behavioral patterns whose form has been hardwired into our brains by millennia of inherited experience. When they appear in dreams, they generally reflect a similar presence in your waking life, as well as your gut reaction to it, or else suggest a need for the incorporation of the characteristics that they represent into your waking existence. The unconscious may similarly recruit other symbolic figures to appear on the dream stage in wish-fulfillment and warning dreams.

Amazon/Huntress

The amazon represents the feminine principle in its intellectual and practical form. She can be symbolized by a successful professional woman—a fierce competitor who may be much more focused on her career than she is on her romantic and/or family life. The amazon's dark side is the huntress, who ruthlessly stalks her prey—be it someone or something that she desires—only to spit it out and discard it after she has had her way.

Symbolic and Verbal Associations
› Intellect
› Practicality
› Power
› Competition
› Stealth
› Female sexual aggression

Positive Interpretations: If you are female, did you dream that an armor-clad and sword-wielding warrior woman came to your defense at a company meeting in which you were being ignored or otherwise mal-treated by your male coworkers? If so, did you relish your feelings of vindication and triumph as your her-oine unleashed chaos, ruin, and defeat upon your enemies? Perhaps, even, you found yourself trans-formed into an amazonlike warrior, whose power and stealth struck fear into the very souls of those who oppose you? If so, then your dream may have served a dual function: both to fulfill your desire for success, authority, and/or revenge, and to hearten you in your real-world struggle to advance your career. Your dream need not have been so dramatic, however: the amazon may appear in a variety of forms and guises— even in animal form—and any time that your dream highlights a powerful, self-assured female, then you should consider whether the amazon has paid you a nocturnal visit. If you are a man who dreamed of the amazon, she may have represented an actual woman in your waking life, or else your need or desire for a strong female companion or influence.

Negative Interpretations: Did you have a dream that highlighted the amazon-gone-bad? Perhaps, in your dream, you were being chased by a sinister female predator who chilled you to the very soul with her evil war cry? If so, was your assailant someone who was recognizable from your waking life? It may be that your unconscious conjured the image of the huntress to alert you to someone who is attempting to hurt or even destroy you for her own dark ends. And, especially if you are a woman, you may want to consider whether you yourself have been acting the part of the huntress. The huntress is also associated with sexual aggression, and she may appear in your dreams as an overly forceful female suitor, especially if you are male.

Anima

For men, the anima is a personal female archetype: she is the "soul image"—not a mirror image, but the reverse of one's self, which is one of the reasons why the anima (and the animus, for women) is manifested as a member of the opposite sex. For example, if you are a shy, inwardly drawn man, your anima might take the form of a gregarious, outgoing woman.

Symbolic and Verbal Associations
› A mirror image of one's self
› A man's feminine qualities
› Positive or negative aspects of one's character
› Emotional, intuitive, or empathetic impulses
› Internal gender balance

Positive Interpretations: If you are a man who dreamed of a woman who was very different from yourself, you may have had a glimpse of your anima. And if this is the case, the details of your dream and your reaction to your anima will help you to interpret the reason why your unconscious sent her your way. For instance, perhaps you are a conventional, somewhat conservative, man who dreamed that a youthful, carefree woman approached you at a party and asked you to dance with her—something that you would never dream of doing in the real world—then how did your dream self react? If, in your dream, you threw off your old inhibitions and allowed yourself the freedom and enjoyment of dancing with your anima, then the message from your unconscious is fairly clear, and it is that you might find that you are happier and have more fun in your life if you would loosen up some of your self-controls and allow yourself to act in a less inhibited way more often. In general, any time that you dream of your anima, your unconscious mind may be trying to tell you that you need to counterbalance your overriding male tendencies or behavior. For many men, the appearance of the soul image may signal that they have been ignoring their emotional, intuitive, or empathetic impulses, for instance. Following the example of your anima will usually help you to develop into a more balanced, happier person, and it is likely that it will also fortify and improve your relationships with women.

Negative Interpretations: A man's anima is the outline of his feminine side; as such, his anima was originally based on the example set by his mother (or by a motherlike figure in his life), although it eventually expands to encompass the characteristics of all of the women whom he has come to know in his life. And depending upon the nature of these female influences, the anima may be either positive or negative in character. When the anima is negative, she will often share qualities with one or more of the principal negative female archetypes: the terrible mother, the siren, the huntress, and the witch. (Please see the individual entries for these archetypes.)

Animus

The animus is a woman's "soul image": a male archetype that represents the reverse image of herself, which is one of the reasons why the animus (and the anima, for men) is manifested as a member of the opposite sex. For example, if you are a spontaneous, somewhat reckless, woman, your animus might take the form of a cautious and reserved man.

Symbolic and Verbal Associations
› A mirror image of one's self
› A woman's masculine qualities
› Positive or negative aspects of one's character
› The intellect, practicality, and confidence
› Internal gender balance

Positive Interpretations: If you are a woman who dreamed of a man who behaved quite differently from yourself, then you may have been visited by your animus. And if so, the details of your dream and your reaction to your animus will help you to determine why your unconscious summoned his presence. Perhaps, for instance, you are a reserved and withdrawn woman who dreamed that a confident, outgoing man offered to show you around the big gambling casinos in Las Vegas. How did your dream self react? Did you take him up on his offer, and were you surprised to find yourself in fantastic spirits as you learned how to place bets at the blackjack tables? If so, then the message from your unconscious is fairly straightforward: if you would allow yourself to be less inhibited and more outgoing (perhaps if you would sometimes take more of "a gamble" on life), then you might find yourself to be happier and having more fun. In fact, whenever you dream of your animus, your unconscious mind may be trying to tell you that you need to counterbalance your overriding female tendencies or behavior. For many women, the appearance of the soul image may signal that they would benefit from striving to become more confident, pragmatic, or intellectually focused. Following the example of your animus will usually help you to develop into a more balanced, happier person, and it is also likely to strengthen and enrich your relationships with men.

Negative Interpretations: Because the animus is the blueprint of a woman's masculine side, it was originally modeled on the example set by her father (or by someone who acted as a father figure in her life), although it eventually expands to encompass the characteristics of all of the men whom she has come to know in her life. And, depending upon the nature of these male influences, beginning with the father, the animus may be either positive or negative in character. When the animus is negative, it will often share qualities with one or more of the principal negative male archetypes: the ogre, the wastrel, the villain, and the black magician. (Please see the individual entries for these archetypes for a detailed description of their characteristics.)

Authority Figures

Typical authority figures include police officers and judges, teachers and professors, doctors, heads of state, spiritual authorities (such as priests and rabbis), parental figures (traditionally the father), and even referees and umpires. When they appear in our dreams, it is usually for one of three reasons: to rebuke us for some transgression (whether it is of thought, word, or deed); to act as our advisor or guide; or to warn us that we may be abusing our own authority.

Symbolic and Verbal Associations

› The law; reprimands and punishment
› Spiritual, intellectual, and social lessons
› The example of one's "elders and betters" as advisors and guides
› The voice of one's conscience

Positive Interpretations: Did you dream that you sat in an austere university lecture hall, listening in rapture as a professor talked about the evolution of humans? And did you awake feeling surprised because, in reality, you've never gone to college and you've had very little waking curiosity about science or evolution? Your unconscious might have summoned the authority figure of the professor in order to provide your mind with some much-needed intellectual stimulation—and also to encourage you to seek out more knowledge-expanding experiences in your waking life. Or did you dream that a doctor had hooked you up to a heart monitor and was taking your blood pressure? If so, have you been placing yourself under too much stress and strain lately, so that your health may be in jeopardy? And if your dream doctor advised you to get more rest and to exercise more, then you should probably consider doing just what your "internal physician" has recommended. Or did someone important, such as the king of England, come to a dream tea party that you hosted? And were you delighted when His Majesty praised you for your elegant décor and for the high quality of the tea and cakes that you served? If so, your unconscious mind may have been compensating for your perception that you are unappreciated by others in your waking life.

Negative Interpretations: If you are a Roman Catholic, did you have a dream in which you went to confession and the priest reprimanded you for not having visited your mother in a very long time? If you have you been feeling guilty about your lack of attention to your mother, then your unconscious probably summoned the dream priest to advise you that visiting her would bring you peace of mind. Finally, did you find your dream self in a position of authority? Perhaps you were dressed in the robes of a judge, and you were presiding over a case against your best friend? If so, what was he or she accused of doing? And do you feel that your judgment was fair? If not, your dream may have been a warning that you have been unfairly condemning your friend in the waking world.

Leaders

In a perfect world, our leaders would be those who have in mind the best interests of the people, and they would care for us and guide us much as a good mother or father would their children. In the world that we live in, however, this is sometimes, but not always, the reality, and dreams that involve a leader can be symbolic of the father or mother archetype in either their positive or their negative aspects.

Symbolic and Verbal Associations
› Direction and control
› Wise and just rule
› Royalty and ceremony
› The symbolic "father" or "mother" of a nation
› Tyranny and dictatorship; abuse of power

Positive Interpretations: Did you wake up from a dream in which the head of the United Nations called you into her office for a special meeting because she wanted to ask your advice about the state of affairs of the world? If so, your dream may have been an unconscious validation of your waking feelings of intelligence and competence (although it could have been compensating for your feelings of inadequacy, as discussed below under Negative Interpretations). If you dreamed of a leader or monarch, it is also possible that this person represented someone who has power over you in your waking life, such as your boss—and if you think that this may be the case, the person's behavior in your dream will probably either reinforce or compensate for the way that he or she treats you in the real world. For instance, did you have a dream in which your usually cold and unsympathetic supervisor was transformed into your state governor, and did he take you aside and tell you what a good job you've been doing and ask you if there was anything that you would like to see changed? Alternatively, were you moved by a dream in which you listened to the famous civil-rights leader the Rev. Dr. Martin Luther King Jr. give a speech about love and fairness? Sometimes when we dream of a leader, this can be a signal that we should try to develop this person's qualities within our own self.

Negative Interpretations: Did you have a dream in which the country had been taken over by a power-consumed madman who was threatening to spread his tyrannical and cruel control over the entire planet? Your dream autocrat may have represented someone in your waking life who is behaving in this despotic way, or he may have been a messenger bearing a warning from your unconscious that you yourself have been acting the part of the tyrant. Finally, dreams of being singled out by someone famous, including an eminent leader, may be an unconscious attempt to both compensate for and boost a low sense of self-esteem.

Persona

The word "persona" comes from the Latin word for an actor's mask. Each and every one of us has a persona: it is the face that we present to the world. In fact, people usually have more than one version of the persona, each carefully tailored to suit its intended audience, be it one's family, friends, colleagues, or strangers. Most people's personas have one thing in common, however: they are almost always meant to portray their "wearer" in the most positive light possible.

Symbolic and Verbal Associations

›   The personality that one presents to the world
›   Image; character
›   Disguises and masks
›   "False face"
›   An aspect of oneself that is concealed

Positive Interpretations: When we dream of altering our appearance, this is likely to be an unconscious reference to our persona, the personality that we present to others. Did you have a dream in which you put on a disguise? For instance, perhaps you dreamed of putting on a mask that made you look much older than you really are, which caused others in your dream to treat you with much greater respect and deference. If so, and especially if you awoke with good, positive feelings, then your unconscious may have sent you the dream in order to advise you that you should take on a new persona in order to help you achieve your goals. For instance, using the dream example above, it may be that you have been thinking of running for some political office, such as on the city council, but you are much younger than any council member who has ever been elected. Your dream of donning a mask that made you seem older may be an indication that you should take steps in the waking world to make yourself seem more adult—perhaps by dressing more maturely, or by behaving in a more self-assured manner.

Negative Interpretations: Did you dream that you were standing in front of the bathroom mirror at your office, desperately trying to scrub off the clown face paint that you wore? If so, do you feel that you have been "playing the clown" for your coworkers—when, in reality, this is against your true nature? Your dream was probably a warning that your clownish image is in conflict with your true, inner self, and that you would be happier and more comfortable if you would cast off this "false face," at least to some degree, and show your coworkers that you also have a very serious, matter-of-fact side to your character (which may be a necessary step in order for you to receive that promotion that you really want, which would give you many more responsibilities than your current position holds).

Shadow

The shadow is an archetypical character that is individual to each person. Usually appearing in the form of someone who is the same gender as you are, the shadow is the representation of all of those qualities that you find particularly loathsome in others—such as, for example, violent aggression, cowardice, bigotry, or unfaithfulness. And though you may despise these qualities, they exist, to some degree, within the character of each and every person, including yourself. Because your unconscious mind probably does such an excellent job of repressing your shadow, its one and only outlet may be the dream world.

Symbolic and Verbal Associations

› The polar opposite of the persona
› Any quality that you despise in others
› Repulsion
› Cowardice
› Hatefulness
› Bigotry
› Brutality

Positive Interpretations: If you dreamed of your shadow, it will do you well to remember that although your conscious mind is prejudiced against the qualities that your shadow demonstrated, they are not always bad in and of themselves. In fact, if you would take the cue from your unconscious and allow these qualities more of a presence in your waking personality (either by consciously acknowledging them or by embracing them, even), then you might find that your creativity and your joy of life would be greatly enhanced. For example, did you dream of someone—perhaps someone who looked somewhat like yourself—who embodied the very trait that you hate the most: physical aggression? If so, perhaps you would benefit from finding a physical outlet for your own pent-up frustrations, such as kickboxing or karate.

Negative Interpretations: Sometimes the traits that we most abhor in others are those traits that we ourselves have to struggle most fiercely to contain. By fixating our loathing on others who possess these qualities, we can pretend that the qualities do not exist within our own psyche. And sometimes, when you dream of your shadow, the symbol of everything that you loathe within yourself, it can be a sign from your unconscious that these very qualities that you hate are threatening to bubble over in your conscious, waking life. So if you are a young woman whose pet peeve is people who gossip, and if you dreamed of a young woman of about your age who stunned and upset you with the haphazard way in which she slandered her friends and enemies with equal fervor, you may want to consider whether you yourself are the one who has been telling tales behind the backs of your friends and cohorts.

Strangers

When our dreaming mind focuses in on a stranger, it usually has an agenda. Dream strangers often represent some aspect of our character, or of a real-world relationship, that we either have not consciously acknowledged or that we have neglected. This is why they seem unfamiliar or "strange." When interpreting the meaning of a dream stranger, it is very important to consider how the stranger looked or behaved, and how our dream self reacted to him or her.

Symbolic and Verbal Associations

› Someone or something that is unfamiliar or alien
› A newcomer
› A mystery
› An unacknowledged aspect of one's own character
› A threat

Positive Interpretations: Dream strangers often appear as the "embodiment" of our anima (if we are a man) or our animus (if we are a woman)—an archetype that is the reverse image (and the opposite gender) of ourselves. If you are a man, did you dream that an unknown woman knocked on your door and begged you to take her in and help her because she had just been beaten up and robbed? If so, your unconscious may have sent your anima in order to alert you that someone in your life has been hurt (though not necessarily physically) and to call on you to access your nurturing, caring, feminine qualities in order to help this person. Or if you are a woman, did you have a dream in which a strange man rode up to you on his motorcycle and invited you to climb on for a sightseeing ride through the countryside? If so, your animus may have been a messenger, sent from your unconscious to urge you to embrace the outgoing, masculine side of your personality that longs for adventure and excitement.

Negative Interpretations: Did you have a dream in which you and your spouse found yourselves locked in a prison cell guarded by a jailor whom you did not recognize? The stranger who was your dream jailor may have represented an aspect of your marriage—a problem the two of you have ignored or not acknowledged—that is somehow "locking up" your relationship and preventing it from growing or moving forward. If you can remember what "crime" you were being imprisoned for, this may be a clue as to the nature of the problem. (And if, in your dream, you and your spouse worked together to defeat the jailor, then your unconscious may have been encouraging you to work together to overcome the issue or problem in the real world.) Finally, if you dreamed of a stranger who behaved in a way that caused you to feel contempt for him or her, you may want to consider whether this person was actually your shadow, a character who represents the qualities that you particularly despise in others (but that probably exist, to one degree or another, within your own psyche).

Tricksters & Clowns

A wild, rebellious maverick, the trickster (or clown) rejoices in overturning the status quo and causing chaos wherever he roams. This archetype, neither completely positive nor completely negative, is represented in mythology by the Greco-Roman gods Hermes and Mercury and by the Norse Loki. He is analogous to the king's fool: a seemingly capricious prankster who is actually the bearer of much wisdom—and, as such, his appearance in our dreams should be a matter of immense interest to us.

Symbolic and Verbal Associations

› Pranks
› Shapeshifting
› Rebellion; wildness
› Mockery
› Anarchical behavior
› Sabotage

Positive Interpretations: Did a red-nosed clown cavort across the stage of your dream, just as you were making a speech before a large audience about the importance of upholding traditional morality? And did this clown steal the attention of the crowd as he berated and mocked the "moral" issues about which you spoke? If so, your dream trickster was most likely a representation of the inner aspect of yourself that believes that you have become too conservative and narrow in your views—sent in by your unconscious on a daring mission to sabotage your dream speech in order to shake you up and (presumably) out of your boring conventionalism. And—though he may have annoyed, angered, or even embarrassed your dream self—if you heed the trickster's message, you may find yourself transformed into a happier, more open and carefree person.

Negative Interpretations: Did you awake in a sweat, having had a nightmare in which a black-clad anarchist was chanting "Down with schools and education" as he poured gasoline all over your neighborhood's elementary school and lit a fire? If so, the anarchist was almost surely a form of the trickster, who is ever challenging those traditions and values that are held in society's highest esteem. But what purpose could your unconscious have had in sending this criminal maverick to upset your nocturnal slumber? It may be that someone in your waking life— perhaps even yourself—has "gone rogue" in his or her battle against the status quo. If you think that it might be you, you should ask yourself if you have been allowing the ends to justify your means. Perhaps it's time that you re-evaluated your methods before some serious, irrevocable damage is done to yourself or others.

Warrior/Villain

The archetypical hero of myths and legends, the warrior is the mature man whose strength, valor, and conviction have led him to victory after victory on the battlefield. In the language of dreams, he represents positive action. The warrior's arch enemy is his dark side: his own nemesis, the villain.

Symbolic and Verbal Associations
› The hero
› Courage and valor
› Conviction
› Physical strength
› Harmful intent
› Criminality

Positive Interpretations: When the warrior makes an appearance in your dreams, this is often a signal from your unconscious that you need to play the part of the warrior in your own life and take necessary, positive, and decisive action in order to achieve a desired goal. For instance, did you have a dream in which you looked on as a knight in armor, his sword raised high over his head, turned his horse and rode off across a field of battle? If so, do you know what he was fighting for (or against)? Perhaps he bore a special symbol on his shield. Think about the details of your dream, and try to draw parallels with your waking reality. Is there some issue, problem, or hurdle that you have been deliberating whether to "take on"? If you can pinpoint the thing that your dream was referring to, then this should help to clarify the action that your unconscious mind was prompting you to take. Beyond all else, the purpose of your dream warrior was to fortify your soul with the courage and determination to meet all of life's obstacles head on.

Negative Interpretations: Like all of the archetypes, the warrior has a flip side. When he allows himself to succumb to his own selfish desires, with a disregard for all that is right and good, then the warrior is transformed into his dark alter ego, the villain. And whenever the villain plays some part in the drama of your dreams, the message from your unconscious is almost always clear: "This is the way not to behave!" For example, did you dream that you were on the train, making your way to work, when a masked gunman burst into the train car and demanded that everyone hand over their money and jewelry? If so, could it be that you been somehow acting as the "bad guy," either in thought or in deed? (And if, in your dream, you played the role of the warrior and fought back against the gunman, then you are probably already well on your way to defeating the "villain within.")

Spirituality & The Supernatural

Dreams that revolve around issues of spirituality and religion will usually be colored by your own beliefs and experiences in these areas. They can, however, point toward a need or desire to "rise above" one's day-to-day problems or else to be guided by a "higher" authority. And depending on whether they are negative or positive in tone, dreams that incorporate magical or supernatural beings or events may signify that you do not feel in control in your waking world or that you long for the impossible to become a reality.

Angels

Regardless of their religious association, angels (and also saints, bodhisattvas, and avatars) are perfect beings, the embodiments of goodness and purity. They are not gods themselves, but they do have access to heavenly wisdom, and they are traditionally viewed as being messengers or intermediaries between humans and the divine. Angels are typically represented with wings, which are symbols of transcendence, and haloes, signifying their holiness and divine illumination. And when they appear in the world of dreams, there is generally some spiritual or divine meaning, or perhaps a test of faith, at hand.

Symbolic and Verbal Associations
› Perfection
› Spiritual purity and goodness
› Transcendence

› Holiness; divine illumination
› Otherworldliness

Positive Interpretations: In general, when our dreams are graced by the presence of an angel, a saint, or a similar being, the meaning probably has to do with goodness and the quest for spiritual betterment—qualities to which we should try to aspire. As you slept, did you feel that you were being blessed and protected by your guardian angel? If so, this may have been an unconscious affirmation that you have made a correct choice or decision, or that you have been behaving in such a way that is righteous and good. However, sometimes the message that a dream angel brings can be relatively straightforward. If you are familiar with Christian teachings and you dreamed of St. Michael, the angel who cast the rebel Lucifer out of heaven, could it be that your unconscious mind was telling you that there is some negative person whom you would do well to eject from your waking sphere? (For instance, perhaps the new boarder in your house has been plaguing you and your family with his loud music and parties, his bad attitude, and his general disregard for the rules that you have set.) Finally, dreaming of an angel or a similar being may be a sign that you are opening up to a higher level of spiritual consciousness. If you are unsure as to the meaning of the angel's appearance, try meditating on your dream; this may help you to gain new spiritual awareness and insight.

Negative Interpretations: If you were visited by a dream angel, he or she may have brought you a message from higher up (whether you believe the message to have come from the divine, from your unconscious, or from both together). Did the angel warn you that you have made some transgression of thought or deed? If so, you will probably want to consider whether you should take a more ethical position with regard to some issue that you are struggling with in your waking world.

Devils

In Christian lore, devils and demons were originally fallen angels. Cast into hell for their rebellion against God, they now owe their allegiance to the devil (also known as Satan, Lucifer, Beelzebub, and Old Nick). These demons retained their supernatural powers, however, which they now use to tempt and torment humankind. If you dreamed of the devil or his wicked cohorts, this does not signify that you are hurtling toward damnation. Everyone who has ever lived must navigate the convoluted course between good and evil, and sometimes our own personal demons can be viewed as messengers: unconscious warnings that we are in danger of straying from the trail of righteousness.

Symbolic and Verbal Associations
› Evil; malevolence
› Immorality
› Hell; darkness

> Temptation
> Unhappiness; misery

Positive Interpretations: Were you perplexed by a dream that featured a devil or demon because you feel that you are an ethical, decent person who strives for goodness in everything that you do? Perhaps, in your dream, a demon had latched onto your back and, no matter how hard you fought, you were unable to shake him off. If so, your dream may not refer to your current life at all. Instead, the dream demon may have been summoned by your unconscious to remind you of a past wrong that you committed that has never been corrected. (For instance, did you borrow money from your brother many years ago—so long ago that you both seem to have forgotten that you never paid him back? Now that you have consciously acknowledged the debt to your brother, the demon that you dreamed of may continue to harass you until you have settled the matter.)

Negative Interpretations: Did you awake from a fantastical nightmare in which the devil and his cohorts were dancing around your bed in celebration of their conquest of your eternal soul? If so, is there something in your waking life that you are feeling unsettled or guilty about? Perhaps you have been considering whether to take an action that you feel is not quite right, but that would bring you some immediate benefit at the expense of others. Your dream devil may have been a warning from your unconscious that you are in great danger of falling into the spell of an evil temptation that, in the end, will lead you to your own unhappiness. It is also possible that a dream that involves devils or demons is an alert to an external threat rather than a reference to a demon that skulks inside of you. Could it be that you have unconsciously detected negativity from someone in the real world? If you think that this is the case, you will probably want to pay close attention to the message of your dream, and to be on your guard when you are dealing with this person.

Ghosts

If the popular movies are any measure, Western culture is obsessed by the idea of ghosts. Perhaps the allure has to do with our curiosity about the unknown, and our anxiety about what happens to us when we die. If you dreamed that you received an ethereal visitor, you may have been left quite shaken, and trying to determine the unconscious reason for your dream may help you to feel more at peace with your experience.

Symbolic and Verbal Associations

› A loved one who has died
› Nostalgia for the past
› Guilt over wrongdoings
› Fear of the unknown
› Shadows and darkness
› Incubi and succubi

Positive Interpretations: Did you dream that your beloved grandfather, many years dead, walked into the room with you and began talking to you as if nothing was out of the ordinary? And did you feel no fear—and were you, in fact, comforted by your dream? If so, it is likely that your grandfather has lately been on your mind. Maybe his birthday is coming up, or perhaps the anniversary of his death; or maybe you saw someone on the street who resembled him in some way. Whatever the explanation, you will probably be reassured by knowing that your dream is a sure sign that your grandfather remains very close to your heart. And if, in your dream, your grandfather gave you any advice, then he may have been acting in the role of the archetypal wise man, and you will probably want to pay close attention to what he told you.

Negative Interpretations: In your dream, did you cower under the covers in an attempt to conceal yourself from whatever shadowy phantom had found its way to your bedside? If so, did you recognize the specter? Or did the spirit say or do anything that has some association with someone in your present or past waking world? You may want to consider whether your visitor represented a source of guilt that you are feeling—either a person whom you feel that you have wronged or a "ghost" from your past that continues to haunt your conscience. Or, while sleeping, did you feel as though a great, unmovable force was crushing your chest so that you could not move and you could barely even breathe? In times past, when sexual pleasure was taboo, people who had erotic dreams were said to have been attacked by a sexually voracious incubus (a male demon) or succubus (a female demon). Today, the words "incubus" and "succubus" are still used to describe the nocturnal sensation of a weight pressing down on one's chest, together with a feeling of dread and an inability to move, a phenomenon that dream experts think may be due to temporary breathing difficulties combined with sleep paralysis (which we all experience while sleeping, but which we rarely become aware of).

Gods & Goddesses

As divine archetypes, gods and goddesses are eternal symbols of the spectrum of human emotions and experiences. As such, their symbolism is timeless, transcending the partitions of culture and geography. Throughout the ages, gods and goddesses have been said to use their powers to manipulate and control the lives of mortal humans—sometimes for a greater good, and sometimes for their own self-serving reasons. So if you dreamed of a god or a goddess, you will want to take into account any associations that you have with that particular deity when you are attempting to interpret your dream.

Symbolic and Verbal Associations

› Divinity
› The male and female archetypes
› Raw energy; human emotion

> Creation
> Law and order

Positive Interpretations: Throughout history, the characteristics of many gods and goddesses have been shared from culture to culture, and many deities have nearly identical counterparts that are called by a different name. For instance, the Canaanite Ba'al, the Greek Zeus, the Roman Jupiter, the Celtic Taranis, the Vedic Indra, the Hindu Vishnu, the Germanic Donar, and the Norse Thor all share the predilection of hurling thunderbolts to demonstrate their divine discontent. They are all archetypes—symbolizing emotions and experiences that are so universal as to render their base meanings ageless and unchanging. Are you a man who dreamed that you were being courted and seduced by a stunningly beautiful goddess of love? If so, you may have encountered Venus or one of her many counterparts. In fact, even if you do not recognize or know the name of the specific god or goddess that you dreamed of, you will probably recognize the emotions that he or she represents. And if you think that you may have dreamed of a deity, but you are unsure, if necessary consult the male and female archetypes described in the last chapter to see if you can recognize your dream god's or goddess's role and, ultimately, understand his or her message.

Negative Interpretations: As discussed above, the gods and goddesses of the world represent the full range of human emotions, including those emotions that we tend to think of as being negative, such as aggression, jealousy, anger, and vengeance. So if you dreamed that you were trembling in fright before a divine, wrathful warlord, do you find your hostile male supervisor so intimidating that your fear is affecting your ability to do your job? Or if you dreamed of the Greek goddess Hera, who was ever consumed by jealousy over her husband, Zeus, could it be that you yourself have fallen into the lap of that green-eyed brute?

Heaven & Hell

More than anything else, dreams of being in heaven or hell usually refer to your current feelings or state of mind, in that you have probably been finding your life particularly heavenly or hellish of late. You may be relieved to know that such dreams are not predictive of where your soul is destined to spend the afterlife—if you believe in this form of life after death.

Symbolic and Verbal Associations
› States of mind
› Hopes and fears for the future
› Paradise
› Damnation
› Something very good, or "heavenly"
› Something that is outstanding (i.e., "one hell of a racehorse")

Positive Interpretations: Did you have a dream in which you were relaxing in the luxury of heaven, however you imagine heaven to be? Your dream version of paradise may have looked a lot like your favorite vacation destination. Maybe you found yourself upon a bright, tropical island with warm, glittering beaches filled with colorful parrots and coconut trees. If you did have a dream such as this, and if you have been feeling as though you are "in heaven" in the real world, then your dream was most likely mirroring your current state of mind, and affirming what you already know: that life is good. However, if you find yourself perplexed by such a dream because your life, as of late, has been anything but good, then what could have been the meaning of your dream vacation in paradise? It is possible that your unconscious sent you this sort of dream as a wish fulfillment, to make up for the current lack of bliss in your life, and also to hearten you to remember that life can, indeed, be good.

Negative Interpretations: Did you have a dream in which you found that you had died and gone to hell, where the devil and his army of demons were planning to do nasty, tortuous things to you? If so, there are two likely explanations for your nightmare, and only you will know which of the two is more probable. The first is that you are feeling guilty about some wrongdoing that you have committed (or that you have been tempted to commit) in the real world. And if you think that this explanation is valid—particularly if you are wracked with guilt over whatever you may have done—and if you have recurring dreams of this sort, then "righting" your "wrong" may be the only way for you to find peace in dreamland. The other possible explanation for dreams of this type is that, for whatever reason, your current waking life feels like a living hell, and in sending you the nightmare, your unconscious mind was simply mirroring your waking reality (and, perhaps, attempting to prompt you to do something about it).

Magic, Rituals & Spells

In folklore, magical spells and rituals have often been cited as the cause of human good luck, as well as misfortune. However, unlike the type of magic worked by gods, demons, or fairies, rituals and spells are usually said to be the works of some member of the human community. And when magic rituals and spells feature prominently in your dream, an all-important clue as to the meaning of your dream will have to do with the identity of the magician.

Symbolic and Verbal Associations
› Wizards and witches
› The occult; hidden mysteries
› Being "bewitched" or "charmed" by, or "enchanted" with, someone or something
› Control; power
› Curses and blessings
› Psychic attacks and defenses

Positive Interpretations: Did you have a dream in which you were imbued with wonderful powers of magic? Perhaps, in your dream, you found yourself casting a magical circle, pentagram, or hexagram (all symbols of protection) on the earth, while chanting some ancient spell, which you knew was causing your lottery-ticket number to become the jackpot winner? If so, and if you wish that you could magically make yourself rich in the real world, then you probably experienced a simple wish-fulfilment dream—although it is also possible that your dream was mirroring your real-life feelings of vitality and euphoria. Dreams of magical rituals and spells can also be references to our hopes for the future. For example, if you are an expectant mother, did you dream that a magical guardian held your newborn baby in her arms and blessed her? (If so, and if you recognize the guardian, your unconscious may have been telling you that this person may be willing and able to act as your child's protector in the real world.) Or are you a man who dreamed that your girlfriend was brewing a large cauldron full of a magical elixir that was meant to cause you to fall in love with her? If so, your unconscious mind may have been pointing out that you have been "bewitched" or "enchanted" by your girlfriend (in which case, it may be interesting to note that cauldrons symbolize the womb).

Negative Interpretations: Did you have a dream in which your neighbor, with whom you often quarrel, pointed his magic wand at you, over the fence that separates your properties, and turned your prized herb garden into a rotting swampland of weeds? If so, could it be that you have unconsciously detected that your neighbor is planning to do you ill? (And it may or may not be relevant for you to know that, in the language of dreams, wands are considered to be both phallic symbols and conductors of powerful magical energies.)

Miracles

Miracles are what many people call those (usually positive) occurrences that seem to have no other explanation except for divine intervention. In fact, except for their association with religion or spirituality, the idea of miracles is very much akin to that of magic.

Symbolic and Verbal Associations

› The supernatural
› The will of the supreme being or deity
› A reward for piety or goodness
› Religious faith, piety, or devotion
› Something wonderful

Positive Interpretations: Did you have a dream in which something marvelous and wonderful happened to you or to someone else? For instance, if you have a loved one who is gravely ill, perhaps in a coma, did you dream that he or she underwent a miraculous recovery? Or did you dream that your old, beloved, pet dog, who has gone almost entirely blind and deaf, was suddenly able to see and hear as well as when she was a puppy? If so, then you have almost certainly experienced a wish-fulfillment dream. (However, if you are religious, then you may feel that your dream came from whatever deity you believe in, and that it was a sign that your loved one or dog will surely undergo the miraculous transformation of which you dreamed.) Alternatively, did you dream that, by a miracle, the world had been transformed into a planet of peace and love? If, lately, you have been feeling depressed or downhearted because of the dire state of the world's affairs, then your dream may have been sent by your unconscious in order to boost your morale and to give you hope for the future.

Negative Interpretations: The idea of a "negative miracle" may seem strange, but it may help to think of an event that might be called a miracle as being like a "reward" for some people while, at the very same time, it may be a "punishment" for others. A good example is found in the Old Testament of the Bible: when Moses raised his staff to part the Red Sea, this was a positive miracle for the Israelites, but it was surely a negative miracle for the Egyptians from whom they were fleeing, who were swallowed up and drowned by the returning waters. (The same can be said of the biblical story of the plagues on Egypt.) So if you are an avid competitive bowler, did you dream that, just before you were to bowl in a championship game, your fiercest opponent prayed for, and received, a divine miracle that caused your thumb to swell up so large that it would not fit into the hole of your bowling ball? If so, could it be that, deep down, for one reason or another, you feel that you are undeserving of the championship, and that, if justice were served, God would intervene and carry your opponent to victory?

Monsters

As a child, you may have been afraid of the monster that you thought lived in your closet or under your bed, and you may have had nightmares about the fiend's emergence from its lair. Your childhood fear of monsters probably had to do with the fairy tales that your parents may have read to you. But sometimes even adults have nightmares about monstrous beasts. Most dream analysts agree that, in the language of dreams, monsters represent our deep-rooted fears, "ugly" emotions, "monstrous" urges, or painful experiences, problems, or phobias.

Symbolic and Verbal Associations

› Fears and worries
› The unknown
› Danger; a predatory beast
› Evil; dark forces
› Someone or something that is of an exceedingly large, "monstrous" size
› Ugliness; a misshapen form
› Bestial urges

Positive Interpretations: Not all apparent "monsters" are bad, as many, especially modern, fairy tales will attest to. And not all of the emotions that our unconscious might represent as monsters are really unnatural or evil—sometimes, their materialization in dreamland is a sign that they are struggling for self-expression, and the best thing that you may be able to do is to try to come to terms with them. For example, perhaps you are someone who, because of your own internalized bigotry, has been fighting against your attraction to members of your own sex; because of your deep-rooted fears, your feelings of same-sex desire may manifest themselves in your dreams in the form of some monstrous beast. If you can bring yourself to face and accept the "beast" within, you may find that it is not really a monster at all.

Negative Interpretations: Did you have a nightmare in which you were running as fast as you could from a hideous, misshapen ogre that you knew was planning to devour you alive? If so, can you identify your dream ogre with anyone in your waking world? Perhaps there is someone, particularly an older man who might have power over you (such as a boss), whose cruelty and maltreatment of you has turned your daily life into a misery? (And, especially if you are a woman, could your dream ogre have represented a lustful, predatory man whom you feel threatened by?) In another scenario, you may have dreamed that you were being stalked by a blood-sucking vampire. Again, in interpreting your dream, it is important to consider whether you can identify your dream monster with someone in the real world—in this case, someone who might be threatening to "sap your life force" or "bleed you dry." Identifying your dream monster may not only set your mind at ease, it is also likely to bring the nightmares to a halt.

Parallel Worlds

As strange as most dreams are, some dreams are stranger still, especially when we awake with the conviction that we have spent our slumbering hours not resting peacefully in bed, but traveling through a world that was very similar to, but also quite different from, our waking one. Examples of these "parallel-world" dreams include dreams of alien abductions, out-of-body experiences, and lucid dreams.

Symbolic and Verbal Associations

› Escape
› Emotional trauma or upheaval
› Wish fulfillment
› Fear of the unknown, or of death
› Feelings of "alienation"

Positive Interpretations: Did you have a dream in which your consciousness or spirit had left its body, allowing you to soar freely through space and time? Some people believe that these types of exhilarating experiences are actually out-of-body experiences (also known as astral travel or projection). Many people report having had these sorts of experiences during times of physical or emotional trauma or illness. Whether you believe that you had an out-of-body experience or that it was only a dreaming fantasy, it was likely to have been an indication that, for whatever reason, you are now in need of an escape (even if temporary) from your current reality. In a similar vein are lucid dreams. You have probably, at some time or another while you were sleeping, suddenly become consciously aware of the fact that you were dreaming. Most people wake up when this occurs, but it is possible to train yourself to remain sleeping and dreaming, thereby giving you the ability to, at least partially, control your dreams. The ability to have lucid dreams is a powerful tool, which opens up many possibilities—not only for facing your dream "monsters," but also for enjoying wish-fulfillment dreams.

Negative Interpretations: Did you dream that you were visited, or even abducted, by aliens or "spacemen"? When we have a dream that puts our sleeping selves into contact with extraterrestrials, this is often an indication that we feel that we are under threat or attack from "alien" forces. Though it probably won't be easy, if you can bring yourself to begin a dialogue with these "alien" influences—either in the dream world, in reality, or in both—then you may be able to come to understand them, thereby helping to alleviate your fears of the unknown. Another possible explanation of dreams involving aliens is that you feel that you have become "alienated" from those who were once close to you, such as your friends or your family. Again, in this instance, you may be able to assuage much of your anxiety by cultivating better communication with those whom you feel alienated from.

Prophets & Saints

Prophets and saints may be most likely to appear in our dreams at moments of deep spiritual crisis. Because they are traditionally considered to be divine messengers, or intermediaries between the supreme being and humans, their function and symbolism is similar to that of angels—the main difference being that those who believe in prophets and saints believe that these divinely blessed figures were once mortal, flesh-and-blood human beings (unlike their angelic counterparts).

Symbolic and Verbal Associations

› Divine guidance
› A messenger
› Universal truth
› Higher spiritual awareness
› Someone who is a "false prophet"

Positive Interpretations: Did you dream of a prophet or a saint who has a spiritual significance for you? For instance, are you a Buddhist who dreamed of Gautama Siddhartha, a Muslim who received a vision of Muhammad, a Christian to whom Christ or the Virgin Mary appeared, or a Jew who dreamed of the Messiah or the prophet Elijah? If so—no matter what your specific spiritual beliefs are or which saint or prophet your sleeping mind conjured up—the fact that your unconscious mind summoned a symbol of such great significance to you indicates that you may be in the midst of a profound spiritual crisis or crossroads in your life—and you were probably deeply affected by your dream. Have you been feeling particularly anxious about some important decision that you are being called upon to make, perhaps a decision that is so big that it is likely to change the course of your life? If so, it is advisable that you listen closely to the message that your prophet or saint brought to you because, as a conduit of divine wisdom, this spiritual guide is likely to represent your best interests. And even if you are not religious, or if you dreamed of a spiritual figure of a religion that is not your own, do not simply dismiss your dream messenger as being a "false prophet" as your unconscious probably understands that all religions share some part of the universal truth.

Negative Interpretations: If you dreamed of a prophet or a saint, did he or she bear a message of warning regarding something that you feel sorry for or embarrassed about (i.e., some transgression that you have committed, or some "faulty" aspect of your personality)? Again, as above, you will want to consider the point that your spiritual guide bore; his or her dream manifestation may be an unconscious prompt that you are ready to make a change in your life, and to ask for, and receive, absolution for your "sins." Or, finally, could your dream saint or prophet's appearance have been an unconscious attempt to balance out the fact that your waking life is largely lacking in spirituality?

Religious Ceremonies

If you dreamed of an elaborate religious ceremony, you may have been comforted, unsettled, or puzzled—depending upon your religious background and feelings, which must be taken into account when you are attempting to interpret your dream, as well as the setting and any religious paraphernalia that was involved. And although the primary significance of such a dream will often accord with your own particular religious education and beliefs, it is also true that some interpretations are fairly universal, even for atheist dreamers.

Symbolic and Verbal Associations
› A request for divine assistance or intervention
› A religious congregation or community
› Joy; an uplifting experience
› Enlightenment
› Healing; renewal
› Mystical transformation
› A stagnant ritual or tradition, lacking in spiritual vitality

Positive Interpretations: If you had a dream in which you were chanting, singing, or reading some sacred scriptures, or if you dreamed that you heard any of these things, then this may have been a signal from your unconscious mind of your desire to receive a divine answer to some question (which may be of a spiritual nature). Or did you have a dream that you were watching or participating in some religious ceremony or rite with which you are very familiar? For instance, if you were raised as Roman Catholic and you dreamed of lining up to receive the Holy Communion, how did this make you feel? If you felt comforted, blessed, or uplifted, then, depending on your current religious practices, your dream may have been a reflection of your sense of security and joy because you feel that you are living in accord with the moral code that you believe in, or else of your desire to reconnect with your religious background. And it may be interesting to note that dream chalices, which enclose the water of life (as well as, for some Christians, the blood of Christ), may reflect how you see yourself and your potential in the world. (So was your dream chalice made of gold and jewel-encrusted? Or was it a humble pewter cup?)

Negative Interpretations: Did a dream in which you were witnessing a religious ceremony kindle your feelings of anger, rejection, or rebellion? If so, then your unconscious mind may have been pushing you to break away from convention and assert your individuality (which is possibly being stifled by a rigid belief system or moral code). Or if you dreamed that you were praying fervently, perhaps tearfully, it may be that you are in search of some divine or spiritual advice, assistance, or intervention to help you with a troubling problem or dilemma.

School & Work

If you spend a large proportion of your waking hours at school or work and found yourself in the same environment in dreamland, the setting per se is not likely to have had much symbolic significance, reflecting as it did merely your daily reality. If you are no longer a student, however, with what do you associate your schooldays? Is there a lesson that you consciously need to relearn, perhaps? And if you do not have a job, would you be happier "working at" something in the real world, or are you feeling "slave-driven" or "bossed around"?

Deadlines

If your waking life is filled full of plans and deadlines, then the pressure that you are under may also plague you in your dreams—thereby disturbing your sleep time (which may be the one and only time that you have to relax) and also, perhaps, signaling that you may be close to breaking point.

Symbolic and Verbal Associations
› Feeling hurried or rushed in one's life
› A sense that "time is running out"
› Unresolved issues; things left undone
› Motivation; action
› A feeling of being "under pressure"; a need to relax
› A desire for excitement or intellectual stimulation

Positive Interpretations: Were you thrilled or galvanized by a dream in which you had one hour to produce a research report on some topic of interest to you? For instance, have you always had an interest in astronomy, and did you dream that you were charged with compiling a report for N.A.S.A. on the most recently discovered stars in our galaxy? If so, it may be that you are craving intellectual stimulation, and that you would benefit by enrolling in school or by making more time in your life for reading and study. Or if you have been working on a long-term project (such as writing your memoirs or compiling a family history) and you dreamed that a deadline for completion was drawing near, this might have been an unconscious attempt to spur you into action so that you might finally finish your project.

Negative Interpretations: Did you have a dream in which you realized, with panic, that you had to produce a ten-page paper by the following day, which you had not even begun to research? If so, are you under an exceptional amount of stress in the waking world, so that you feel that you are beginning to lose control over your life and your work? It may be that you are so much "on the go" and are filled with so much anxiety during your waking hours that you are unable to give yourself permission to relax even in the dream world. In addition, it is possible that your dream may have been your unconscious's way of trying to tell you that there is something in the real world that has slipped from your conscious mind—perhaps a work deadline or an upcoming meeting that you must prepare for. And if you had a dream in which you were working yourself ragged, but with the over-all feeling that you were accomplishing nothing at all, could it be that you have taken on so many tasks and responsibilities during your waking hours that you are not really doing justice to any of them? If so, you may benefit from delegating or letting loose of some of your responsibilities, which would both allow you to do a better job on the duties that you retain and give you a greater peace of mind.

Examinations

If you dreamed of preparing for, or of taking, an examination, the most important factor in determining the meaning of your dream is probably how it made you feel (i.e., nervous, anxious, pleased, proud, etc.). These sorts of dreams often have to do with our feelings of self-esteem and self-worth, and are likely to reflect our feelings with regard to our relative success or failure in the "testing" situations that life often brings.

Symbolic and Verbal Associations
› Performance anxiety
› Fear of failure
› Hopes for success
› Trying or "testing" situations
› Feelings of self-esteem and self-worth

Positive Interpretations: Did you dream that you were sitting in a large lecture hall, a sharpened pencil in hand, and that you felt confident and eager as your professor passed out an examination paper and instructed you to begin? And as you answered the questions one by one, did you find that you knew the material so well that you were sure that you would receive 100 percent? A dream of acing an exam is likely to have been an unconscious statement regarding your positive self-esteem and confidence in your brains and abilities. And if you do have an exam or test looming in the real world, your dream may serve as a confidence-boost—an unconscious effort to reassure you with regard to your performance ability and to cheer you on to success. It is important to note that the real-world exam or test that your dream was alluding to need not be a test or exam in the traditional sense, but could be a "testing" or trying situation that you must deal with during your waking hours.

Negative Interpretations: Did you have a dream in which you were sitting in a classroom, sweating and panicking as your teacher passed out an exam paper because you had forgotten to study and were completely unprepared? If so, there are a few possible explanations for this sort of nightmare. First of all, if you had a dream such as this and you have a real examination coming up soon, then your dream may have been a reflection of your anxiety and fears with regard to how you will fare. And, as discussed above, under "Positive Interpretations," it is important to remember that your dream may have been drawing a parallel not with an actual exam, but with a difficult or "testing" situation in the real world. But if there is no examination or other sort of trial looming in your near future, then you may want to consider whether you are suffering from low self-esteem, or whether you feel that you do not measure up to your peers or are unable to do things as well as most other people (i.e., general performance anxiety). A similar interpretation may apply if you dreamed that your teacher handed you back an exam paper marked with an "F." (For more on this, see the associations for *Failure*.)

Failure

Though dreams of failing are not likely to be predictive of the actual outcome of a real-life test that you must undergo, or of a feat that you must accomplish, they may indicate how you feel about your relative chances of success. This type of dream may also be an unconscious reflection of your general feelings of worth or inadequacy, or else of your hopes and fears for the future.

Symbolic and Verbal Associations

› Feelings regarding one's relative worth or inadequacy
› Shame
› Preoccupation with, or worries with regard to, waking problems
› Measuring oneself against others
› Competition and rivalry

Positive Interpretations: Did a dream that cast a spotlight on a past failure give you a new, positive perspective on the incident? For example, did you dream about that second-grade spelling bee that has haunted you for years—the one you lost at the very last minute, when you misspelled a word that you knew well because you were nervous and you answered too quickly? But, in your dream, instead of breaking down into tears, running from the stage, and locking yourself in the restroom for an hour, as you did in real life, did you calmly acknowledge your loss, shake hands with the winner, and happily accept your trophy for second place? If so, then your dream may be a sign that you have finally moved beyond your pain and that—even more importantly—you have discovered a valuable real-world lesson about dealing with loss. On the other hand, if you dreamed of failing an exam or some other challenge that you must soon face in the waking world, then you can rest assured that your dream was not necessarily predictive of how you will fare in reality. Instead, your dream may have been an unconscious attempt to explore how you would feel and what you would do if you did fail, thereby helping you to prepare for the possible worst.

Negative Interpretations: In your dream, did you revisit the horrors of some past failure, which caused all of the terrible feelings and heartache that you felt at the time of the incident to return in full? If so, and especially if this is a recurring dream, it may be that you have not resolved your painful feelings from this incident and, as a result, have been unable to learn from your experience and move on. Also, whether your dream highlighted an actual (past) or a hypothetical failure, you may want to consider whether your dream might have been an indication that you are suffering from feelings of low self-esteem or worth. Alternatively, if you dreamed that you received an "F" for a real-world exam or that you somehow failed a trial that you must soon undergo, then your dream may be a sign that you are not yet as primed as you should be (in which case, your unconscious may have been attempting to push you into action).

First Day

The first day of kindergarten, school, college, or a new job is usually some combination of exciting and terrifying—and if your dreaming mind carried you back in time to a first day of school or work, it may be that you are in the midst of another big life change that is causing you to feel as insecure and uncertain as you did on the day that featured in your dream.

Symbolic and Verbal Associations
› Loneliness
› Uncertainty; confusion
› Insecurity and anxiety
› Excitement
› Life changes

Positive Interpretations: Did you dream that you were a small child, once again heading into the classroom for your first day at school? If so, have you recently started working in a new job, moved to a new city, or had some other major life change? Your dreaming mind may have conjured up your past experience of the first day of school in order to mirror your reaction to, and your feelings regarding, your current life change. So, in your dream, how did you feel? If your dream self felt excited, happy, or anxious to get started with your lessons, then this bodes well for how you are feeling about your new job, home, or other life change. An exciting dream about the first day of school may also indicate that you are feeling bored or dull in your current life, and that you long for the opportunity to stimulate your intellect through learning, to be trained in a new skill, or to develop a natural talent.

Negative Interpretations: Did your dreaming mind cause you to relive a past first-day-of-school trauma in which you felt highly insecure, apprehensive, lonely, or fearful? In your dream, did you weep and run from the classroom, back into the arms of your mother as she attempted to depart the school? If so, and if you have recently undergone a major life change (such as a change of employment or residence, as discussed above), then your dream has been an indication that you are feeling uneasy in your new situation. It may be that you are unsure of how to behave in your new environment, that you are worried and uncertain about what others expect of you, or that you are simply feeling lonely because you miss your old friends or colleagues and because you haven't yet formed any real friendships in your new situation. Having this type of dream may also be a sign that a childhood insecurity about being judged or derided by your peers, or even shunned by others, has been reawakened in the real world. For instance, have you recently been feeling as if you are the brunt of the jokes around your office? Or have your former friends at work treated you coldly ever since you took a public stand against a company policy that you felt was wrong?

Graduation & Promotion

Graduations and promotions are milestones in our lives, when we are recognized for our achievements and when we officially move upward, from one level to the next one. As such, they are occasions of pride and celebration. Having a dream that highlights a graduation or a promotion may be an unconscious reflection of the fact that you have completed one phase of life and that you are moving on to the next one, though it may also indicate that you wish to be publicly recognized for your efforts and accomplishments.

Symbolic and Verbal Associations
› Recognition for hard work and accomplishments
› The end of a life stage
› New beginnings
› Pride and joy
› Success and opportunities

Positive Interpretations: Did you dream that you were dressed in the cap and gown of a graduate, and that you felt a great swell of pride and emotion as your name was called out and you rose, amidst clapping and cheering, to receive your diploma? Or did you have a dream in which your boss publicly congratulated you for your good work, shook your hand, and welcomed you as the newest junior executive of your firm? If you had any dream of this sort, might your unconscious mind have called up the image of a graduation or a promotion in order to mirror a culmination or a new beginning in your waking world? For instance, have you recently made some important accomplishment, received a promotion at work, or moved on from one stage of life to the next (e.g., have you recently closed the deal on your first home, or were you recently married)?

Negative Interpretations: If you had a happy dream of receiving a promotion or of graduating from an educational program, and if, in your waking life, you are feeling disgruntled, discontented, or unrecognized for your efforts and accomplishments, then you may have experienced a wish-fulfillment dream (in which case, your unconscious mind was giving you a taste of the attention, recognition, and public acclaim that you so desperately crave in the real world). However, if your dream depicted you being recognized for some accomplishment that you have not yet completed, but that you plan to complete in the future, then your unconscious may have been attempting to urge you to do so. For example: if, in your dream, you were receiving your PhD diploma, this may have been an unconscious prompt for you finally to finish writing that dissertation that you've been dragging out for so long. Finally—particularly if you can draw no immediate parallel with a major life event or change in the real world—it is also possible that your dream signified a desire on your part to take some positive action, such as enrolling in college classes or launching a new project at work.

Interviews

Whether they go well or poorly, interviews tend to be highly stressful situations, and a dream of sitting for an interview is likely to be stressful as well. You may ask why your dreaming mind would choose to put you through such an ordeal. Though the answer will depend on the specific details of your dream, any dream of sitting for an interview or of otherwise being put on the spot is liable to be reflective of your self-image and your feelings and anxiety about how others perceive you.

Symbolic and Verbal Associations
› Self-image; persona
› Nervousness with regard to new people and situations
› Anxiety about how one is perceived
› Opportunities
› Challenges or tests
› Fear of failure

Positive Interpretations: Did you have a dream that depicted you sailing through an interview smoothly and confidently? And do you have an interview coming up in the near future? If so, your dream may have been an unconscious attempt to prepare you for the interview and to reassure you about your ability to perform well and to make a good impression on the interviewer. In general, any dream of performing well when put on the spot may also be an indication of your general feelings of confidence and security regarding your social and intellectual abilities. However, because we generally go to interviews in order to better ourselves in some way (for example, to attend a new school or to seek a better job prospect), having a dream such as this may also be a sign that you desire to pursue new and better opportunities in your life.

Negative Interpretations: In your dream of sitting for an interview, did you fumble nervously through your briefcase, drop your pen and papers into a pile of disarray, and stumble and stutter for the correct words to say as you felt the sweat collect on your forehead and begin to soak through the armpits of your suit jacket? Or did you dream that you were in the audience of a comedy-club show, when the comedian suddenly singled you out to come up and be his "assistant"? And, in your dream, did you begin to shake with fear and dread as the spotlight shone on you and the crowd began to clap and call for you to ascend to the stage? Dreams like this usually highlight some waking worry or angst, either regarding a specific situation that you must face or a general anxiety about how you are perceived by those whom you may regard as your superiors. (Most people feel this sort of social anxiety from time to time, but if you have recurring dreams of this sort, you may want to consider whether you have a more serious issue with your self-respect.)

Lessons & Learning

When you are attempting to interpret the meaning of a dream that placed a focus on a past event or lesson that you learned, it will be helpful for you to try to draw a parallel with your current life as it is highly probable that this past event or lesson has, once again, become relevant to your waking world.

Symbolic and Verbal Associations

› A hunger for knowledge and intellectual stimulation
› Revisiting or relearning lessons from the past
› New methods of problem-solving
› Personal potential; abilities
› A need to expand or broaden one's mindset

Positive Interpretations: Did you have a dream in which the major focus was on a particular lesson that you were learning? If so, in attempting to interpret your dream, it will help to consider the dream lesson in the context of your past, present, and future. For example, did you dream that you were listening with excitement to a lecture about the American Revolution—a subject that you have long been interested in, but have never pursued to your fullest desire? If so, and particularly if you have been feeling frustrated by a lack of intellectual stimulation in your life, your unconscious mind may have been encouraging you to pursue your historical interest (perhaps by enrolling in a class or by reading more history books in your leisure time). Any dream of learning or studying a subject of interest to you may be an unconscious reference to your unrealized personal aptitude, talents, or abilities (thereby prompting you to nourish them). It may also be that knowledge of the particular subject that you were studying in your dream may be of help to you in solving a current real-life problem. Alternatively, if you had a dream of learning about a subject that is unfamiliar to you, such as a foreign language, this might have been an unconscious sign that you would benefit from expanding or broadening your mindset, or attempting to view or understand the world from other people's points of view.

Negative Interpretations: Did you dream of relearning a lesson that was taught to you long ago, but that you have long since forgotten or put out of your conscious mind? For example, if you dreamed of learning the fundamentals of English spelling and grammar, have you become sloppy in your written communication, so that your letters and e-mails are full of badly worded sentences and spelling errors? If so, could your unconscious mind have been reminding you of your English lessons in order to encourage you to review those important rules of the language so that you might make a better impression on your business colleagues with whom you communicate in writing (which will, in effect, better your career prospects)?

Teachers & Bosses

Like all of the adults whom we encounter in our early lives, our teachers have the power to make a strong impression on us—one that can be very good or very bad, or something in between, depending on how they used, or abused, their power over us. The "stamp of authority" that they place on us may leave a deep impression on our unconscious mind, to emerge later in our dreams.

Symbolic and Verbal Associations

› Worries with regard to one's personal worth, or how one measures up (as judged by an authority figure)
› Nostalgia for happier times
› Unresolved pain or anger
› Vulnerability and humiliation
› Misuse of authority; an ogrelike figure
› Respect and obedience
› Resentment and rebellion

Positive Interpretations: In your dream, was your mind agreeably cast back to your old classroom, where you found yourself once again standing before, and conversing pleasantly with, your most favorite teacher of all time? If so, it may be that your unconscious was giving expression to your feelings of nostalgia for that time in your life. Another possible explanation for a dream such as this is that your memories of that early, loved teacher have been triggered by someone in your current life—perhaps your boss at work, who has earned your respect and your obedience because of her kindness and patience. Or if you are in a position of power with regard to others, a third explanation is that your dream was an unconscious reminder for you always to treat your subordinates with dignity and with compassion.

Negative Interpretations: Did you have a dream in which you found yourself face to face with a former teacher whom you feared and hated, and did this dream teacher berate and humiliate you in the same nasty way that he or she did when you were a child? A dream like this may signal current real-life insecurity, perhaps sparked by a hostile or overbearing boss, or by a similar set of circumstances in your current life. It is also possible that you have never really come to terms with the pain and suffering that you experienced because of this cruel teacher, and perhaps you are still very angry at this person—in which case, your dream was probably a signal that this is a good time for you to reassess this painful experience, and to think about it from an adult perspective so that you may be released from the hurting and begin to move past it. But if none of these interpretations ring true, is it possible that you yourself have been acting the part of the cruel monster in your dealings with others, possibly the people who work under you?

Anxiety Dreams

Anxiety dreams are among the most commonly remembered, probably because, in a sort of vicious cycle, they feed the very fears of which they are an expression, fears that the conscious mind often tries its utmost to suppress. Some dream experts believe that consciously and rationally identifying, facing, and dealing with the often irrational worries and insecurities that give rise to such recurring nightmares will banish them from your sleep.

Betrayals

Betrayals have been the fodder of drama and tragedy through the ages. The idea of betrayal is made much more sinister by the fact that, in order to betray someone, the betrayer must first have that person's trust—so, by definition, we may only be betrayed by a friend or loved one. There is no doubt, therefore, that in the world of dreams, betrayals are among the most highly stressful of subject matters.

Symbolic and Verbal Associations
› Suspicion
› Loss of trust
› Someone who is "two-faced"
› A turncoat
› Being "stabbed in the back"

Positive Interpretations: Did you have a dream in which you betrayed one of your dearest friends, albeit for good reason? For example, if, in the real world, your best friend has been hiding her drug problem from her family, whom she has been also stealing money from in order to support her habit, did you dream that you "blew the whistle" on her with her family, in order that she might receive professional help for her addiction? If so, your unconscious mind may have been trying to tell you that—although it may cause your friend to become very angry with you—betraying your friend's trust, in this instance, may be the best thing that you can do for her.

Negative Interpretations: Did you awake feeling very angry or embittered because you had a dream in which your best friend "stabbed you in the back," or betrayed your trust, perhaps by telling your most intimate secret to someone else? For instance, in your dream, were you infuriated and deeply hurt when you found out that your best friend, to whom you tell almost everything, had gone behind your back and told someone who is your rival or your enemy a secret of yours that you would never have told anyone else in the world (and, even worse, a secret that is likely to cause you public shame and ridicule if it ever became known)? If so, what could have been the meaning of your dream? If you have no cause to believe that your friend has actually exposed the secret that was featured in your dream, is it possible that your unconscious mind has detected that your friend's loyalty to you may be wavering? Or was your dream a simple reflection of the growing distance that you have felt between yourself and your friend, which you may have internalized as your friend's rejection or emotional betrayal of you? Or, alternatively, are you feeling guilt over some betrayal that you have committed against your friend–a situation that was inverted by your dreaming mind, perhaps to make you feel somehow righteous or blameless for your own disloyalty?

Buried Alive

The fear of being buried alive is widespread and has prompted some fairly extreme practices throughout history to ensure that deceased loved ones are indeed dead before their burial. In the language of dreams, being buried alive may symbolize a feeling of being overwhelmed or overtaken by problems or worries.

Symbolic and Verbal Associations
› Feeling hemmed in or claustrophobic
› Worldly demands, obligations, and worries
› A "black hole" that one cannot climb out of
› A "living death"
› Hostility or anger

Positive Interpretations: In your dream, were you walking through a lush forest, and did you come across a riverbank, where you lay down and gave in to the pleasurable sensation of your body sinking into the soft, warm mud? And, in your dream, were you overcome by a great sense of peace and comfort as the wet soil began to cover your body completely? If you had a dream of this sort, do you feel as if your waking life has become too frantic or frenetic, and do you wish that you could "ground" (i.e., calm or steady) yourself, or let go of your waking troubles, if just for a while? And if you had a dream in which you willingly went to your grave, do you wish that you could undergo a symbolic death and therefore be "reborn" as a "new" person?

Negative Interpretations: Did you have a terrible nightmare in which you found yourself trapped inside a dark, deep, earthen hole, with soil being thrown over your head so that you were being slowly, but surely, buried alive? And no matter how hard you tried to claw your way out, did your dream self seem to sink deeper and deeper into your grave? If you did have such a dream, you were probably deeply disturbed and mystified as to why your unconscious mind would subject you to this nightmare experience. The most likely interpretation for this sort of dream is that the demands, obligations, and worries of your waking life have become so overwhelming to you that you feel as if you were at the bottom of a "black hole" that you are unable to climb your way out of. If this is the case, and if you feel as if your life has become like a "living death," then you may want to consider seeking the help of a professional counselor. In a slightly different scenario, did you have a dream in which someone was deliberately burying you alive? If so, who? If it was the star player on your rival bowling team (for instance), then your unconscious mind may have been trying to force you to recognize the deep hostility that this person has for you, and his or her wish to see your goals and ambitions "dead and buried."

Chases

Perhaps one of the most common and universal anxiety dreams is that of being chased. When interpreting a dream of this sort, it is important to try to identify who (or what) you were fleeing from, and to try to draw a connection with a person or a thing (perhaps even something within yourself) in the waking world.

Symbolic and Verbal Associations
› Escape from danger
› Fear of one's inner urges or traits
› Suppressed feelings; guilt
› Hostility
› Unsolved problems

Positive Interpretations: If you had a dream in which you were being chased by someone whom you did not recognize, it is possible that your pursuer was actually your shadow: a quality or an aspect of yourself that you are anxious to escape or to hide from. (This may be particularly true if your dream pursuer's appearance was repulsive to you and if he or she was of the same sex.) If so, what was it about him or her that frightened you so much? Was it his or her sadness, greed, or lust? Whatever your shadow represents, your unconscious may have been telling you that it is time for you to acknowledge and come to terms with this aspect of yourself.

Negative Interpretations: Did you awake with your heart pounding and your body soaked with sweat after having had a dream in which you were being hunted or chased by someone or something? If so, can you remember who or what you were running from? Was it a person whom you know in the real world? Or was it an unknown pursuer? A ghoul or monster? Or a vicious wild animal? Your dream is a likely indicator that you are feeling threatened by someone or something in the real world, and the answer to the previous questions will tell you who or what you feel threatened by—be it an actual person, a situation, or something that lies within yourself. For instance, if you dreamed that you were being chased by your mother-in-law, do you know why you might feel threatened by her? Has your unconscious assessed that your mother-in-law (or perhaps your wife's entire family, which your mother-in-law represents) disapproves of you and seeks to undermine your marriage? Or, in your dream, did your boyfriend transform himself into a werewolf and chase you for hours on end? And did you somehow know that he was planning to tear you into shreds and then eat you? A dream such as this may signify that you are feeling overwhelmed or dominated by your overbearing boyfriend, perhaps even more so because he has been pressuring you to make a commitment to marriage. However, unless you know that they represent someone whom you know in the real world, nonhuman dream pursuers usually symbolize an internal fear or need (an "animal" instinct) rather than an external threat.

Drowning

In symbolic terms, dreams of drowning may indicate overwhelming trouble or problems, or a conflict with one's environment (including other people), so that there may be a feeling of "swimming against the tide," being out of one's "emotional depth," or struggling to keep one's "head above the water."

Symbolic and Verbal Associations

› Being "over one's head" in trouble, etc.
› Conflict, as in "swimming against the tide," or struggling "against the current" (of opinion, etc.)
› A desire to "go with the flow"
› Being out of one's "emotional depth"
› "Treading water"; trying to keep one's "head above the water"
› Being in need of help, or a "lifeline"

Positive Interpretations: Did you have a dream in which you were miraculously saved from drowning when someone threw you a rope and pulled you up into their boat? If so, did you recognize the person who tossed you the "lifeline"? Your unconscious may have been hinting that he or she has the ability to throw you an "emotional lifeline" in the real world, thereby saving you from your own inner turmoil, which is threatening to swallow you up. Alternatively, in your dream, did you find yourself becoming exhausted and giving in to the idea of drowning—only to discover that the moment you stopped fighting the water, you began to drift gently and peacefully downstream? If so, your dream may have signaled an unconscious desire to stop fighting some real-world battle and instead just to let yourself "go with the flow."

Negative Interpretations: Did you have a nightmare in which you were fighting for your life as you struggled against a mighty current of water? If so, have you been battling the "current" of popular opinion, or "swimming against the tide" in the waking world? Or, in your dream, were you swimming in the ocean when you drifted too far away from the shore, so that you were out of your depth? If so, are you out of your "emotional depth" in the real world (perhaps because you have gotten romantically entangled with someone who is already married, or because your girlfriend is sending you contrary signals regarding her feelings for you)? And if, in your dream, you found yourself desperately thrashing and flailing about, trying to keep your head above the rough and tossing waters, are you inundated with problems in the real world, so much so that you feel that you are beginning to lose all emotional control? (In other words, are you so distressed by your current waking situation that you fear that you may be headed for a nervous breakdown?)

Embarrassment

Embarrassment is the base of many different types of anxiety dreams. Generally speaking, dreams of being embarrassed may signify insecurity, and a fear of appearing foolish in public or in front of someone whom the dreamer wishes to impress.

Anxiety Dreams

Symbolic and Verbal Associations
› Insecurity
› Exposure (of private thoughts, feelings, etc.)
› A fear of looking silly or foolish
› Public shame

› Inappropriate behavior, or fear of acting inappropriately

Positive Interpretations: In your dream, did you commit some act or error, or find yourself in a situation, that caused you public embarrassment? For instance, did you stand up to deliver a speech with food stuck between your front teeth? If so, when your folly became known to you, did your dream self feel embarrassed, yet deal with the situation gracefully? For instance, in your dream, did you laugh along with everyone else and make a joke about the food in your teeth, and then move on smoothly to the more serious topic of your speech? If so, your dream may have been an unconscious affirmation that you are able to take the jokes and punches that life throws your way, and that you are a fairly confident person who is usually able to hold your own in tricky situations.

Negative Interpretations: Did you have a dream in which you did something that caused everyone around you to laugh at you, so that you turned hot and red-faced with utter embarrassment? For instance, did you dream that you were walking through the cafeteria at your work, with your lunch tray in your hand, when you slipped and fell, scattering your tray and food everywhere? And, in your dream, did your coworkers roar with laughter, while not one single person bothered coming over to help you as you attempted to pick yourself up and clean up the mess? This sort of dream is likely to indicate that you feel insecure (particularly in the presence of your coworkers), and that you fear doing things that will make you appear silly or foolish in public. If so, asking yourself why you are feeling insecure will help you to move toward laying your fears to rest. Or if you had a dream in which you were embarrassed in front of someone in particular, who was the person? Do you feel a fervent desire to impress this person in the waking world, and if so, why? (For instance, perhaps you harbor unacknowledged romantic feelings for him or her.) Finally, if your dream had to do with an embarrassing public exposure of your private thoughts or feelings, were they something that you feel shame about in the real world? If so, why? Your dream may have been an unconscious signal that it is time for you to come to terms with whatever it is that you so desperately wish to keep covered up.

Falling

While dreams of falling are quite common, we may have these types of dreams for a number of different reasons. Sometimes there is a purely physiological trigger for a dream of falling. These dreams may also reflect a conscious fear or phobia of heights, which may or may not have been rekindled by something in the waking world. Other times, dreams of falling may point to anxiety with regard to failure.

Anxiety Dreams

Symbolic and Verbal Associations

› Insecurity
› Fear of losing control, or of "letting yourself down"
› Fear of failure, or of "falling down"
› "Falling from" grace, fame, power, etc.
› "Falling for" someone; "falling" in love
› A conscious phobia of heights

Positive Interpretations: If you have a great fear of heights in the real world and you had a nightmare in which you were dangling over a deep chasm as you clutched onto the side of a cliff, your dream may have been simply reflecting your waking phobia (particularly if you recently watched a movie about mountain-climbing or if you are planning to go hiking in the hills). Another common dream of falling occurs as people are just going to sleep: as you were "falling" asleep, did you dream that you were walking along a road and that you suddenly slipped into an empty hole? If so, you probably experienced a type of muscular spasm known as a myoclonic jerk (which sometimes occurs during the hypnagogic state, before we are fully asleep), and your unconscious reacted by incorporating it into your dream. Finally, is it possible that your dream was triggered by your real-life experience of "falling for," or "falling" in love with, someone?

Negative Interpretations: Perhaps the most disturbing of falling dreams are those that our unconscious mind uses to alert us to our insecurity or fear of losing control, failing, or "falling down" in some aspect of our lives. In these cases, the details of your dream can help you to determine the specific meaning. For example, if you dreamed that you were in danger of plummeting from the top of a skyscraper, the skyscraper was probably a metaphor for your high expectations of yourself (or the high expectations that others have for you). Perhaps you are afraid of "letting yourself down," or of your career "coming to a fall." If none of these interpretations seem likely, then you may want to ask yourself whether there is something in the real world that you are clinging to as if it meant life or death, perhaps because you are afraid of letting it go. In your dream, what happened next? Did you lose your grip and actually fall? If so, and if your dream self hit the ground, you may have been surprised to find that there was no real damage done to you—thereby indicating that the real-world "fall" that you are afraid of may not be as bad as you have anticipated.

Imprisonment

Dreams of being confined or imprisoned are often a reflection of our real-life frustration at not being able to do as we please or to reach for our ambitions or our potential. In interpreting dreams of this sort, it is helpful to take a look at who (or what) was imprisoning you.

Symbolic and Verbal Associations
› Feeling confined or restrained
› The inability to reach one's fullest potential

› Someone who is "boxing you in"
› Being "locked into" (or trapped within) a situation, such as a relationship
› Self-imposed emotional constraint

Positive Interpretations: Did you have a dream that depicted you breaking out and escaping from a jail or a prison? If you did, in your dream, as you ran farther and farther toward liberation, did you feel a great sense of joy and thankfulness welling up in your heart? If so, you may have been perplexed by your dream (unless, of course, you are an inmate in a real-world prison, in which case your dream was probably a form of wish-fulfillment). By casting you in this sort of dream scenario, your unconscious was probably prompting you to set yourself free from whatever it is that is keeping or holding you back in the waking world; for more on this, see below, "Negative Interpretations."

Negative Interpretations: Did you dream that you were locked in a dark, dreary cell, with only a small window for sunlight to come through, and your only furnishing being a tiny, old prison cot? If so, you probably felt extremely lonely and/or frustrated, which may be how you are feeling during your waking hours (which is probably why you dreamed such a thing in the first place!) In general, dreams of being locked up or restrained usually signify that you are feeling frustrated because someone or something is preventing you from acting freely or from realizing your aspirations or your fullest potential in the waking world. In your dream, did you see your captor? If so, who was it? Is this person "boxing you in" in the real world? Are you being forced to live according to someone else's rules or plan? Or are you feeling "locked into" or trapped within a waking situation, relationship, or responsibility from which you feel you cannot escape? It is also possible that your imprisonment is self-imposed. Have you been constraining or hiding your emotions in order to protect yourself from emotional hurt or to prevent others from getting too close to you? Did the bars of your dream prison stand for your own inhibitions? Whatever the case, your unconscious was probably highlighting your feelings of confinement in order to urge you to break free from whatever it is that is holding you back—be it your own emotional inhibitions or else a deadening or draining job, a bad or stifling relationship, or a hefty commitment that is taking its toll on you. Is it time that you face down your fears and take a long-awaited taste of freedom?

Kidnappings

Dreaming that you have been kidnapped may signify feelings of being trapped or emotionally restricted. However, dreaming that you have kidnapped someone else may mean that you are trying to contain or inhibit some aspect or aspects of that person (perhaps within yourself), or else that you are trying to force your will or your opinions upon them.

Symbolic and Verbal Associations
› Feeling trapped or controlled; emotional restriction
› The desire to inhibit or contain aspects of oneself
› A diversion from your goals
› Holding onto something that it would be better to let go
› Forcing one's views or opinions on someone else

Positive Interpretations: If you dreamed of a kidnapping, were you the victim, the kidnapper, or merely a witness? If you had a dream in which you had kidnapped someone else, did you know the person? Who was it? And what qualities or characteristics do you associate with this person? Especially if your victim was the same gender as you, your unconscious may have cast this person in the role of your shadow—the polar opposite of the persona that your ego has constructed, which embodies all that you find irritating and loathsome in others (and in yourself). Your dream of kidnapping this person may have been symbolic of your desire to suppress his or her qualities within yourself. And if you think that this may be the case, then your dream was probably an unconscious cry for you to acknowledge and face up to your shadow, and perhaps consciously to embrace that part of yourself that you have thought of so negatively. However, if this explanation seems unlikely, you may want to ask yourself whether you have been trying to force your views or your will on someone. If so, do you desire to control this person because you have developed an unhealthy romantic infatuation with him or her, or because he or she embodies something that you desire? It is also possible that your victim represented something in your life that you are holding onto, when you would perhaps be happier if you could let it go.

Negative Interpretations: Did you have a dream in which you had been kidnapped? If so, there are a number of possible explanations. Do you feel trapped or controlled by your dream captor in the real world? For instance, was your dream self kidnapped by your ex-husband, who continues to bully and control you even though you are no longer married? Or was your dream kidnapper someone who distracts or diverts your attention from your waking goals and ambitions? Another possible interpretation is that your kidnapper represented some force or situation that you feel is victimizing you in the real world. This may be your own beliefs or views on life, which may be so rigid that they are restricting your personal growth.

Lost

If we think of life as a long, zigzagging road, as it often seems to be, then it is easy to see how a dream of being lost may pertain to one's loss of direction in the waking world. This may have to do with the dreamer's goals and ambitions, important decisions, or with personal identity or beliefs.

Symbolic and Verbal Associations
› A loss of direction in life
› A lack of goals

Anxiety Dreams

› Confusion
› The need to get "back on track"
› A murky sense of personal identity

Positive Interpretations: Did you have a dream that depicted you wandering through the wilderness, hopelessly lost and afraid? And, in your dream, were you relieved and joyful when you found a map that would put you back "on the right track" to known territory? A dream like this may have been an unconscious attempt to hearten you with the knowledge that, although you have recently "lost your way" in life, you will soon find your proper direction once again. A similar interpretation may apply if, in your dream, you observed or followed someone who seemed to know the right way to go. Did you know the person? Your unconscious may have been trying to tell you that he or she is a good example to follow, or else that he or she has good advice to give you.

Negative Interpretations: In your dream, were you terribly frightened to find yourself lost in a foreign city? If so, your unconscious may have been reflecting your loss of direction or focus in the waking world. Have you lost sight of your goals, or strayed from the path that you must take in order to reach them? Or have you given up on your ambitions altogether? For example, are you confused about the next step that you should take on your career path? Or are you unsure of how you want to proceed in your current relationship (be it moving forward, toward marriage, or giving yourself more distance in order to decide how you really feel)? It is also possible that your dream was highlighting your loss of identity or self-knowledge—perhaps because you have recently undergone some major life changes, which have "thrown you for a loop" and changed your "path" in the world, so that you no longer know "who" you are or how you want to live. If this is the case, then thinking about what brought on the changes, or in what ways you have changed (which, therefore, may aid you in discovering the specific nature of your dilemma), will help you to decide "the best way forward." You may find that you have developed completely new goals and ambitions, of a nature that you would have never previously dreamed of.

Unpreparedness

Everyone has had them: dreams in which you walk into class and the teacher is passing out an exam that you knew nothing about. Even worse—your dream self may not even have gone to class all term! Many people have these sorts of dreams even years after they last set foot in a classroom; the universality and sheer terror aroused by this sort of scenario makes it excellent fodder when our unconscious wishes to send us an anxiety nightmare.

Symbolic and Verbal Associations
› Fear of failure
› Feelings of inadequacy

Anxiety Dreams

› An inability to "get it together"
› Self-criticism; low self-esteem
› Anxiety regarding a real-life testing situation

Positive Interpretations: If you have been preparing and studying very hard for an upcoming real-world exam, were you perplexed by a dream that depicted you walking into the exam room completely unprepared? If so, your dream may have simply been giving expression to your worst fears and worries regarding your performance in the exam, as well as preparing you for (though not necessarily predicting) your possible failure. Or did you have a dream in which you completely blew off preparing for your weekly team meeting at work (an event that you happen to loathe in the real world)? And, in your dream meeting, did you sit back and text-message your friends while your coworkers blandly hashed through the boring business at hand? If so, your unconscious may have been allowing you to have a brief reprieve and a bit of fun by sending you a wish-fulfilment dream, though you may also want to consider whether your dream was an unconscious call for you to re-evaluate your career or job choice.

Negative Interpretations: If you dreamed that you were surprised by a test or an exam that you had not studied for at all, this may have been a metaphor for some testing or trying situation that you must face in the real world. Have you taken on, or been assigned, a real-world challenge that you feel unable to meet? Your dream may also point to a general lack of confidence or self-esteem. Do you feel as if you do not measure up to others around you? Of course, if you are a student and you do have a real-world exam coming up, which you have not been studying for as diligently as you know you should, then your dream may have been an unconscious effort to spur you into studying harder. Alternatively, did you stand up to give a dream speech before a group of people, only to realize, with dread, that you had no idea what you wanted to say? And when you opened your mouth to speak, were you even more upset because all that you could do was stammer and stutter? If so, your unconscious may have been highlighting your waking feelings of uncertainty, as well as your fear of scrutiny and criticism.

Wish-Fulfillment Dreams

Wish-fulfillment dreams are generally little treats, compensations, or morale-boosts from you to yourself, especially if your waking existence is currently grim or you are feeling unloved or unappreciated. They may even make you feel so wonderful that they inspire you to work toward recreating the circumstances of your dream in the waking world, in which case your unconscious may have given you a much-needed incentive literally to make your dream come true!

Dream Lovers

In the language of the unconscious, dream lovers may signify a number of different things. In trying to interpret such a dream, the first step is to try to determine who, or what, your dream lover could have represented in the waking world.

Symbolic and Verbal Associations
›   Euphoria
›   Romance
›   Suppressed attraction to someone; repressed sexual desire
›   A need for affection, love, or comfort

Positive Interpretations: In your dream, were you filled with a warm and euphoric rush of feelings because you were in love? If so, who was your dream lover? If it was your real-life partner, whom you are very much in love with, then your dream was likely underlining and reaffirming your feelings for him or her. But if the romance between you and your partner has waned, then your unconscious may have been trying to remind you of the reasons why you fell in love with him or her in the first place—and of the love that you continue to feel for your partner, though it may be suppressed to an unconscious level. And if you think this latter interpretation may be true, then your dream was probably a call to action, from your unconscious, for you to take steps toward rekindling the spark in your relationship.

Negative Interpretations: Were you unsettled or disturbed by a dream in which your lover was someone whom you regard as a mere friend or acquaintance in the waking world? For instance, did your unconscious play out a scene in which you were basking in the loving embrace of your neighbor or a coworker? By sending you this dream, your unconscious may have been trying to alert you to your attraction to this person, though you may consider your feelings inappropriate for one reason or another—which can make this type of dream extremely disturbing, especially if you are already in a committed relationship. So if you think that this interpretation may apply, then your unconscious mind was probably allowing your desires to be expressed in the venue of dreamland, where no actual harm or pain will be caused to anyone. However, if you are in a relationship and yet you continually have sexual dreams about others, then it may be advisable to try to determine the reason or the problem (sexual frustration, for instance) and to work toward resolving it in the waking world. Alternatively, if your dream caused you to view someone in a new, romantic light, then consider whether it is time for you to acknowledge and express your feelings for him or her in the waking world. And, finally, if you dreamed that you were in love with someone, but that your feelings were unreciprocated, are you uncertain of how this person feels about you in the waking world, and are you afraid of being rejected by him or her?

Fame

Almost everyone experiences the desire to be famous at some point in life. We may wish for fame—and also dream of being famous—at times in our life when we are craving more recognition and respect from those around us.

Symbolic and Verbal Associations

› Recognition, admiration, and respect for one's efforts or abilities
› Power
› Success
› Desired personal qualities or characteristics
› The fruits of diligence and hard work

Positive Interpretations: Did you dream that you were famous for some talent or skill that you nurture and take pride in during your waking hours? For example, if you play the cello in a local orchestra, did you have a dream in which you were hailed and celebrated as the very best cello player in the entire world? If so, your dream may have reflected your real-life desire for more recognition of your musical talent, but it may also have been an unconscious call for you to continue your quest to fulfill your highest aspirations for your musical career. And if you dreamed of a real-life famous person, what qualities does this person symbolize to you? He or she may have been acting as your anima (if you are a man) or your animus (if you are a woman), highlighting a personal quality or characteristic that you admire in others and would like to possess yourself, or a quality or characteristic that is relevant to a current life situation you are faced with. (So, for instance, if you dreamed of Mother Teresa, do you wish that you could have more compassion for others, or does a current situation in your waking life call for you to practice self-sacrifice?)

Negative Interpretations: Did you have a dream in which hundreds of thousands of people cheered and called out for you as you were paraded through the streets in a grand limousine? If your dream self savored the adulation that was heaped upon you, this may signal that you feel unrecognized or undervalued by others, and that you crave recognition and admiration from those around you, either for what you consider to be your outstanding personal qualities or for some talent or expertise that you feel you possess. So can you remember what your dream self was famous for? A similar interpretation may apply if you had a dream in which you were greeted or singled out by a famous person whom you admire—in which case, your unconscious was likely attempting to give your self-confidence a boost, if only a temporary, dreamland one. (Yet the effects of your dream may be more long-lasting if you heed the message from your unconscious and take the necessary steps to raise your self-esteem in the real world.)

Heroism

Whenever our unconscious portrays us taking some sort of positive action, it is usually a good idea to heed the dream example and to strive to behave in such a way in the waking world. This applies to dreams in which we find ourselves committing heroic deeds of bravery and/or rescue: the unconscious may be signaling that it is time for an act of bravery (though perhaps in the service of emotional, not physical, heroism) in our waking life.

Symbolic and Verbal Associations
›   A "knight in shining armor"
›   "Riding to the rescue"
›   An emotional "savior"
›   Inspiration to do "good deeds"
›   Guidance and encouragement

Positive Interpretations: Did you have a dream in which you, a "knight in shining armor," were riding to the rescue of an innocent victim who had been taken captive by a villain? Dreams of this sort may be meant to inspire or encourage you to behave in a similarly brave or gallant way in the face of some real-life problem or challenge, even though the nature of the problem or challenge may not be clear to you at this time. Did you know the person whom you rescued? And do you regard yourself as this person's actual or potential "savior" in the real world? Or, in your dream, did someone else ride to your rescue? If so, who was it? Do you regard him or her as your savior in the real world? (It is also possible that your unconscious summoned a heroic archetype in order to inspire you to cultivate these qualities of bravery and courage in your own waking life.) What did your dream savior rescue you from? Answering these questions may help you to identify what element of your life needs rescuing, what is threatening it, and how best to try to save it.

Negative Interpretations: If you had a dream that a hero rescued someone from a villain (and, in your dream, you may have played the part of either the hero or the victim), do you know who the villain was, or who (or what) he or she may represent in your waking world? Is it possible that your unconscious has determined that this person is "up to no good"? Or was your dream a signal that you yourself have been acting the part of the villain during your waking hours? And if you dreamed that a strong and brave hero or heroine rescued you from the clutches of evil, do you wish that a courageous savior would liberate you from a difficult real-world situation? For instance, have you been feeling increasingly uneasy because of your boss's threatening sexual advances, and do you wish that someone (perhaps the company manager) would recognize that you are in jeopardy and would take steps to extricate you from your boss's menacing reach?

Revenge

Dreams of exacting revenge on those whom we feel have harmed us may bring the temporary pleasure of "getting even," and such dreams may also have a safety-valve effect, allowing us to vent our negativity in the safe space of dreamland. However, if dreams of this type recur, this may signal an unhealthy fixation on past wounds.

Symbolic and Verbal Associations

› A grudge; emotional wounds
› "Rubbing it in"
› "Getting even"
› "Revenge is sweet"

Positive Interpretations: In your dream, did you finally take revenge on someone from your past who abused their power over you? For instance, did your dream self travel back to the fourth grade, when your cruel and imperious teacher made your life a misery by singling you out for ridicule day after day? And in your dream, did you lead your class in a mutiny, causing the malicious teacher to cower under her desk? If so, your unconscious was probably compensating for the disempowerment and emotional pain felt by your fourth-grade self by affirming that your adult self would not put up with such treatment. Or did you have a dream in which you were able to "hit back" at someone in your waking life whom you feel has the upper hand and uses it against you? For example, if your father uses money to control your actions, did you dream that you did something to cause him public embarrassment, such as showing up at his birthday party in your underwear? A dream like this may be serving a few functions. For one, it may be an unconscious warning that your father's dictatorial attitude is pushing you to your limits, thereby signaling that you had better find a reasonable way to free yourself from his control. Your dream may also have been serving as a safety valve, allowing you to "blow off some steam" in dreamland so that you won't have as great a need to do so in the real world.

Negative Interpretations: Were you disturbed by a dream in which you took revenge on someone in an exaggerated or extremely violent manner? Did you dream that you went back to your old place of work, from which you were fired, and that you pulled out a shotgun and opened fire on your former colleagues? If so, you probably awoke feeling enormously upset—and rightfully so—but it is important to note that your dream was not necessarily a reflection of your conscious wishes. Instead, your unconscious may have been using the dream to alert you to your feelings of pain and anger, which you may have repressed so well in the waking world that you are not even conscious of them. If, upon reflection, you think that this may be the case, the healthiest course of action is to face up to your feelings, however painful this may be—perhaps with the help of a professional counselor.

Status

Dreams of having an increased status—i.e., being the boss—in either the professional or domestic (or in any) realm of life may mirror a general desire to rise in status in the waking world. Such dreams may also be an unconscious comment on our attitudes and actions within our waking roles.

Symbolic and Verbal Associations
› Power and control
› The person "at the top" or "at the helm"
› Being "in charge" or "in control"
› Someone who is "bossy" or overly pushy
› A tyrant or "ogre"

Positive Interpretations: In your dream, did you find that you had been named as the C.E.O. of the corporation that you work for? If so, how did your dream self feel about being "at the helm"? Did you feel confident? Pleased? Energized? Were you a just leader who sought the best for your company and the people who worked for you? Your dream may be a reflection of your professional goals and ambitions, indicating that you feel that your professional abilities and work habits may potentially lead you to the top of the corporate ladder. Or if you have recently received a real-life increase in your status at work (for instance, if you were promoted to the level of junior executive), then your dream may have been both underlining your new elevation in status and encouraging you to continue following your ambitions.

Negative Interpretations: A dream of being the boss or of being in control or having power over others may also have been a simple form of wish fulfillment—an unconscious signal that you feel unrecognized or undervalued for your work and your abilities. In your dream, how did you behave and feel? Did you have a dream in which you found yourself acting the part of an "ogre" in your role as boss or leader? For example, in your dream, did you assume the position of head of your company and immediately fire all of the people with whom you have ever been in competition, even though they may always have done their jobs very well (which is, perhaps, why they made you feel competitive)? Or, in your dream, did you rewrite the company rules so that no one except yourself could take off any personal time for things like doctor's appointments or special family events? If so, ask yourself whether you've been acting like a tyrant during your waking hours—whether at work, within your family, or in any arena of your life. And if you wish that you had greater status or power so that you could either make yourself feel more important by taking advantage of others, or could take revenge on those you feel have wronged you, then you should consider whether you suffer from low self-esteem or whether you have difficulty controlling and managing your anger.

Vacations

When the unconscious sends our dream selves on vacation, it usually does so in order to urge us to take some time off from our dull or demanding daily routines in order to revitalize our bodies, our minds, and our spirits. This generally applies whether the dream vacation was relaxing or more adventurous.

Symbolic and Verbal Associations

› Rest and relaxation
› Needing a break
› The desire to "get away from it all"
› Adventure
› Peace and tranquility
› Feeling "out of place" in one's environment

Positive Interpretations: In your dream, did you find yourself lazily sunning yourself as you lay back and relaxed, sipping an iced cocktail on a sparkling beach in the Caribbean? If so, have you been feeling worn out, overworked, or stressed out in your waking life? Your dream may have been an unconscious attempt to provide you with a bit of dreamtime relaxation and rejuvenation, as well as to urge you to go ahead and book that vacation that you've been meaning to take for so long now. At the very least, your unconscious was probably trying to encourage you to expose yourself to fresh or "foreign" ideas and influences. Alternatively, did you take a dream vacation of a more exciting type? For instance, in your dream, were you backpacking through the Amazon or traveling on a safari through Africa? Perhaps you were with a team of climbers, making an ascent toward the top of Mount Everest? If you had an exciting dream adventure such as this, and if you are feeling bored with the tedium or monotony of your daily waking life, then your dream may have been your unconscious's attempt to encourage you to reenergize and reinvigorate yourself by adopting a more adventurous lifestyle—not necessarily by climbing Mount Everest, but perhaps by joining a rock-climbing club, learning to snowboard, or engaging in some other exciting activity that you are interested in.

Negative Interpretations: Did you awake feeling bewildered or even frightened because you had had a dream in which you found yourself in a foreign environment? For example, in your dream, did you feel utterly lost and confused—and possibly even threatened—because you could not speak the language or read the writing of the land that you were in, nor could you find anyone who could speak your language? If so, your dream may have been reflecting your feeling of being "out of place" in your current waking environment. In the course of your dream journeys, did you encounter any problems or obstacles?

Wealth

A dream of being wealthy may be a form of simple wish fulfillment, thereby "making up" for a lack of wealth in the real world. However, dream riches may also be a reference to nonmonetary wealth (i.e., the things in life that "can't be bought").

Wish-Fulfillment Dreams

Symbolic and Verbal Associations

› Getting your "just deserts"
› Security and comfort
› Social status; feelings of self-worth
› Things that are of intrinsic, or emotional, value
› Being "rich" in love, friends, and so on

Positive Interpretations: Did you have a dream in which you "struck gold"? For example, in your dream, did you discover that you owned some land that was worth a fortune, perhaps because it contained a vast quantity of underground oil reserves? If so, and if you have indeed recently come into some money in the real world, then your dream was probably an unconscious reflection of the pleasure you have gained from your new real-world wealth. Or if this is not the case, do you feel that you deserve a pay raise at work? (If so, it may be time to ask for one!) However, if your finances (for better or for worse) are the farthest thing from your mind, then it is possible that your dream fortune was a metaphor for wealth of a nonmonetary type. Thinking about the details of your dream in relation to your waking-life situation may help you to decide if this may be the case and, if so, what your dream wealth referred to. For instance, did your dream gold represent a "heart of gold"? And if so, whose? Are you blessed with a "wealth" of love in your life? Do you have a "treasure" of knowledge, faith, or inner strength?

Negative Interpretations: In your dream, were you exulting because you had suddenly landed a fortune—so much money that you knew that you would never need to work or worry about your finances ever again? Dreams of "striking it rich"— especially if you have them often—may point to a preoccupation with monetary problems or issues; dreams like this may serve as a form of wish fulfillment, an unconscious attempt to make up for a lack of financial security (and/or its accompanying social status) in the waking world. Alternatively, did you have a dream in which you were obsessed with the fear of financial ruin? If so, what was threatening your financial security? It is possible that your unconscious was making a reference to some non-monetary resource that you are in jeopardy of losing. For instance, this could be anything that you fear running short of, such as your ambition, your will, your ethics, or your youthful perspective. No matter what your dream loss represented, your unconscious may have sent you your dream in order to urge you to take the necessary steps to secure your resources.

The Emotional Rollercoaster

Many of us suppress our emotions in the waking world, especially extreme ones. We may do so to avoid alienating those around us, or because we are afraid to appear vulnerable, or even because we feel ashamed of our feelings. This means that the only way in which we can "safely" express our true feelings is in dreamland. Dreams that are flooded by a positive emotion may furthermore often be categorized as wish-fulfillment dreams, while those that are blighted by a negative emotion may be classed as safety-valve dreams.

Anger

Dreams of being extremely angry or of fighting or arguing with someone are a likely sign that our waking efforts to suppress our anger are merely relegating it to the deeper levels of consciousness—especially if these dreams are recurring. And, as with any negative emotion that is released in the dream world, it is important to try to determine the source or trigger of your anger.

Symbolic and Verbal Associations
›   Suppressed negativity
›   Pent-up rage
›   Loss of emotional control
›   Violence
›   Uncomfortable or disturbing memories

Positive Interpretations: In your dream, did you finally have the unbridled pleasure of telling your cantankerous and pushy next-door neighbor exactly what you think of her? If so, you probably awoke feeling vindicated and empowered, and then also probably somewhat relieved to know that you did not vocalize your true feelings so bluntly to your neighbor in the waking world—which was likely to be the exact mission of your unconscious! Although many people or things may anger us in our waking lives, we rarely have the freedom to let off some angry emotional steam by exploding with rage, for fear of the consequences. Therefore, any dream in which you reacted with wrath and fury to someone or something may have had a safety-valve purpose, allowing you to vent your rage and frustration in the safe environment of the dream world, where no one will be hurt (either physically or emotionally) and where there are no real or lasting repercussions.

Negative Interpretations: Another interpretation for a dream in which you exploded with rage at someone or something is that your unconscious mind was sending you a warning that you are coming dangerously close to "the edge" and that your pent-up anger is becoming so overwhelming that you are likely to lose control in the waking world. If you feel that this interpretation may be true, then you will probably want to try to remember who, or what, caused you to become so angry in your dream, and to think about ways of beginning to defuse your anger in the real world (such as some sort of peaceful confrontation with whomever or whatever is aggravating you). If you can remember anything that you said (or, more likely, shouted) in your dream, then this may provide more valuable clues about the source or the nature of your agitation. But if you have recurring angry dreams regarding some person or incident from your past, then the unresolved negativity that you are harboring is likely to keep plaguing you in your dreams until you make a conscious effort to face up to your anger so that you may then let it go and move on with your life.

Fear

If you had a nightmare that left you paralyzed with fear, you probably awoke feeling very relieved to realize that it was just a dream, and you may have spent most of the next day trying to push it out of your memory. However, these types of dreams are underlined by our waking fears—which are very real, though perhaps repressed—which are likely to appear in our dreams again and again until we confront and resolve them.

Symbolic and Verbal Associations

› Unconscious fears; phobias
› Something (or someone) that one finds "monstrous"
› Repressed personal qualities or characteristics
› External threats
› A call to action; the "fight or flight" response

Positive Interpretations: If you have a waking phobia of spiders, did you wake up in a panic after dreaming that hundreds of giant, hairy arachnids were crawling all over you? Or, if you suffer from a fear of heights, did you have a nightmare in which you found your-self dangling precariously over the edge of a very high cliff? If so, your dream was probably just mir-roring your waking phobias, especially if something in the real world has recently triggered your fear. And, as scary as your dream may have been to you, your unconscious mind probably selected the night-mare scenario as a "call to action," in order to urge you to confront and conquer your fear. If you have a recurring scary dream, you may find it helpful to tell yourself that when you next have the dream, you will not run from whatever it is that frightens you, be it spiders or boogeymen, but will instead stand and face whatever it is. If you do, you may be surprised to find that the dream consequences are not as bad as you imagined them to be, which will help to allay your fear and hopefully put an end to the dreams.

Negative Interpretations: The unconscious will some-times portray our fears in monstrous form. Did you have a dream in which you were being pursued by a hideous, fanged monster that had run you down and was about to overtake you? If so, the monster was most likely a symbol of something that you fear in the waking world that you feel is threatening to consume you. Doing some free association may help you to figure out whom or what your dream monster rep-resented. Was it your predatory lover? An ogre-like teacher? Your own "green-eyed" beast of jealousy? Could your dream vampire have represented your energy-sapping friend? (Or had you just watched a vampire movie on late-night television?) Once you have identified the source of your fright, you will be better able to arm yourself in order to do battle with whatever it is that is troubling you.

Guilt

Depending upon your background, guilt may play either a small or a large part in how your unconscious encourages you to behave in the waking world. If you dreamed that you gave in to a temptation that you consider to be taboo, then you may have felt very guilty upon waking and reflecting upon what your dream self had done. However, it is important to note that dreams such as this are merely fulfilling our deepest desires and urges, which the conscious mind may be trying to suppress.

Symbolic and Verbal Associations
› Temptation; suppressed needs and desires
› "Immoral" acts; sexual frustration and curiosity
› Being troubled by one's conscience

Positive Interpretations: If, in your dream, you gave in to a temptation that your conscious mind considers immoral, then you probably felt guilty when you awoke. But instead of trying to repress the desire to which your dream self succumbed, you should acknowledge and to try to come to terms with it. In giving your suppressed desire free rein in the dream world, your unconscious may have been trying to point out that the desire may not be immoral, after all. For instance, if your dream portrayed you engaging in a same-sex erotic encounter, and if this made you feel guilty upon waking, consider why you feel this way. Same-sex relationships in dreamland may denote healthy sexual curiosity or refer to an intense emotional relationship.

Negative Interpretations: Sexual infidelities and the transgression of sexual taboos are probably the most common types of guilt-inducing dreams. Did you have a dream in which you were seduced by an attractive and charismatic stranger, and are you happy in a settled and committed relationship in the waking world? If so, you most surely woke up with a sense of guilt. However, in recognizing that your unconscious most likely sent you your dream in order to reflect and fulfill powerful needs and urges that your waking mind has tried to suppress, you may find that your best course of action is to face and acknowledge the problem, which may be sexual frustration or feelings of emotional isolation, and to work to resolve it in your waking life. Alternatively, did you dream that you cheated or "sinned" against someone you love? For example, did you dream that you sabotaged your sister's wedding plans? If so, your conscience may be troubling you about some aspect of your waking feelings or behavior toward your sister, whether or not you are consciously aware of it. For instance, are you jealous of your sister's relationship with her fiancé? The same interpretation may hold true if you dreamed of being punished for some crime, and—whatever your dream crime was a reference to—you may find that your conscience won't allow you any peace of mind (including in your dreams) until you right whatever wrong you feel you have committed.

Happiness

Dreams in which we feel profoundly contented, happy, or joyful are rarer than those in which we are filled with negative emotion, perhaps due to the difficulties we often experience in life and our consequent anxieties about things like our relationships, our livelihoods, and our health. However, the unconscious mind sometimes attempts to bring us a bit of happiness in dreamland, perhaps to comfort and encourage us and to compensate for our waking troubles.

Symbolic and Verbal Associations
› Security, comfort, and contentment
› Wish fulfillment
› Compensation for waking doubts and anxieties
› A sense of wellbeing
› The attainment of one's "heart's desire"

Positive Interpretations: If you dreamed that you were deeply contented or happy, without a worry or a care in your mind, and if this more or less sums up how you feel in your waking life, then your dream was probably merely reflecting your real-life situation and feelings, and you should consider yourself to be a very lucky person! Alternatively, it is also possible that, in sending you your dream, your unconscious mind was attempting to present you with the key to your own real-life happiness. What details can you remember from your dream? Can you recall what made your dream self feel so happy? Was it another person? Being in a certain place? Something you were doing? Once you have identified the source of your dream happiness, then you can consider whether your unconscious was fulfilling a wish that is out of your reach or that is unrealistic in your waking life, or whether the realization of your "heart's desire" may be obtainable if you choose to reach out for it.

Negative Interpretations: No matter how happy we are with our waking lives, most of us are at least somewhat beleaguered by nagging doubts or worries about such things as our relationships, our family life, our careers, our health, politics, the environment, and so on. Has something in the real world been causing you to fret or worry, or are you currently having an unhappy or difficult time in your waking life, and did you nevertheless dream that you were in a blissful state of contentment and wellbeing? For example, are you currently undergoing the stress of getting divorced, which is putting a strain on all the other aspects of your life, and did you dream that you were in a loving relationship and that all of the elements of your life were in complete health, balance, and harmony? If so, then it is possible that your dream was an unconscious attempt to comfort you in compensation for your real-life troubles—and perhaps also to hearten you to carry on in your quest for happiness by giving you a glimpse of what the future could hold for you.

Hatred

We are not likely to dream that we hate someone or something unless we harbor some underlying negativity toward this person or thing in the waking world, whether or not we are consciously aware of our feelings. Therefore, it is important to pay attention when we have a dream in which we are filled with hatred, because this may be the unconscious's way of highlighting trouble in real life.

Symbolic and Verbal Associations

› A negative obsession
› Enemies; conflict
› Anger; unhealed emotional wounds
› Self-loathing; internal struggles

Positive Interpretations: Did you have a dream in which you were so overwhelmed by your hatred for someone that you expressed your emotion in a way that you would never think of doing in the real world? For example, if you really hate your job, did your dream self pour gasoline all over your office building and cheerfully set it ablaze? Or if you can't stand your neighbor's cat, who continually overturns your garbage cans and soils your garden, did you have a dream in which you called in the pound to pick up your feline foe? Any dream in which we commit atrocious acts of meanness or violence against someone or something that we abhor may be serving a safety-valve purpose, allowing us to blow off our steam in an extreme way in the dream world, where no one will actually be harmed and where there are no lasting consequences. Our dream selves having done so, we may find that we are able to cope better and more calmly with our adversaries in the waking world.

Negative Interpretations: Sometimes dreams in which we are filled with hatred are simply meant to reinforce, or to alert us to, our waking feelings of negativity. In such cases, your unconscious may depict you as engaging in some sort of conflict in order to enlighten you with regard to the source and nature of your loathing. Dreams of physically fighting with someone are probably pointing to feelings of hostility, or to a personal conflict or struggle with someone in the waking world. If you were engaged in a dream battle, whose side were you fighting on? And against whom were you fighting (or whom might your enemies have represented in the real world)? Whatever the dream scenario, it is important to try to work out who or what the focus of your dream hatred represented, and what each dream player symbolized in your waking life. And if these dreams are recurring, they may signal an unhealthy negative obsession on your part, in which case you should seek ways to abate your anger or to distance yourself from whatever is upsetting you in the real world. But what if you did not recognize the object of your dream self's hatred? Particularly if it was a person of the same sex as you, consider whether he or she represented some aspect of yourself that you loathe.

Jealousy

Though we may feel jealous for a number of different reasons—whether we are envious of someone's looks, talents, or possessions, or whether we fear that our partner has feelings of attraction for someone else— the bottom line of any dream of being jealous is that we perceive ourselves as being somehow inadequate.

Symbolic and Verbal Associations

› Feelings of inadequacy
› Envy; the green-eyed monster
› Hostility
› Relationship insecurities
› Fear of rejection

Positive Interpretations: Were you surprised by a dream in which you jealously vied for the attention of someone who, in the waking world, is merely a casual friend or acquaintance? For example, in your dream, did you find yourself amidst a party of people, and were you competing with others for the attention of your sister's boyfriend's mother's cousin, a person whom you barely know? If so, your dream may be a sign that you have romantic feelings for him or her, whether or not you have realized or acknowledged these feelings in your conscious mind, or else that you are attracted to some special quality or qualities that this person possesses, and that you wish to develop a closer friendship with him or her.

Negative Interpretations: If you had a dream that placed a spotlight on the fact that you were jealous of someone, chances are that something about this person makes you feel deficient in some way. So, can you identify how? If you were envious of his or her charm or grace, for example, might these be the sort of qualities that you would benefit from nurturing within yourself? Alternatively, you may be able to defuse your feelings of jealousy by accepting and telling yourself that—while you admire such and such characteristics within a certain person—you, yourself, have a multitude of other good qualities that more than make up for your self-perceived shortcomings in this regard. However, if you dreamed that someone else was jealous of you, do you know why they were jealous? Your unconscious mind may have detected that this person harbors hostility toward you in the real world. Finally, did you have a dream in which you felt jealous of someone's hold over the attentions of your real-life partner, or in which your partner cheated on you or actually left you for someone else? If so, your unconscious may have been reflecting your feelings of insecurity with regard to the strength of your relationship or the consistency of your partner's love for you, coupled with a fear of rejection. You need not take your dream as an ill omen, however, unless you have been experiencing serious difficulties in your relationship or you have some actual reason to believe that your partner's affections may be waning or directed elsewhere.

Loneliness

As social creatures, most humans need a fair amount of social interaction in order to be happy. And if we become too physically distanced or emotionally withdrawn (if we are overly fixated on our work, for example), a sense of isolation may creep up on us—perhaps without us even realizing it—and our feelings of loneliness may make themselves known in our dreams.

Symbolic and Verbal Associations
› Emotional distance or withdrawal
› Physical isolation
› Becoming disconnected from family, friends, and other loved ones
› Solitude
› Abandonment; rejection

Positive Interpretations: Did you have a dream in which you experienced utter "aloneness" without feeling lonely? What's more, did you luxuriate in the peace and tranquility that you experienced? If so, is your daily life hectic and strained? Do you wake up before sunrise to get the kids off to school before rushing off to your job, which you do not leave until after sundown, when you then face an endless list of errands, duties, and obligations, not least of which are the running and maintenance of your household? If this sounds familiar to you, then your dream of being alone may have been your unconscious's way of giving you some much-needed downtime, if only in dreamland. And, if the stress and chaos of your life is beginning to get to you, heed the message of your dream and try to work some quality time into your relationships, before you become frazzled and isolated.

Negative Interpretations: Loneliness may present itself in a number of different dreamland scenarios, such as in dreams of being widowed, if you are married in the real world. If you had a dream that highlighted your feelings of loneliness, is this how you are feeling in your waking life? Have you been feeling sad ever since you had your dream, which seems to have uncorked and spilled out the loneliness that you had been keeping bottled up inside you (which you may not even have been previously conscious of)? And if so, do you know why you feel lonely? For instance, have you recently switched to a new job or moved to a new city, where you have yet to form significant bonds of friendship? Or have all of your best friends departed or moved away? Or is your partner "too busy" with his or her career to give you the attention and affection that you need, so that an emotional distance has developed between you? If you are lonely in the real world, then your dream may have simply been a literal reflection of your feelings—and, in highlighting your emotional isolation, your unconscious was probably trying to urge you to connect, or reconnect, with those around you, or to build new relationships.

Love

There are a number of reasons why your unconscious might cause you to dream of loving someone or of feeling loved: the dream may have been reflecting your waking feelings of love, reminding you how intensely you once felt about someone, alerting you to your feelings of attraction for someone, or reflecting a yearning to be in love.

Symbolic and Verbal Associations
› Affection
› Emotional closeness
› Euphoria
› Romance
› Physical attraction; sexual desire

Positive Interpretations: If you had a dream in which you experienced the joy and exhilaration of being in love, or in which you basked in the love and affection of someone else, and if this is how you feel in the waking world, then your unconscious was likely just mirroring your waking good feelings. However, if you had such a dream and you are not currently in love with anyone in the real world, then your dream may have been signaling your longing to love and be loved by someone, and perhaps reaffirming your desire to seek out a mate in the real world. Or, if the passion between you and your partner has cooled, and you had a dream in which you were once again filled with the heady, idealistic love that he or she once inspired in you, then your unconscious may have been urging you to rediscover the romantic excitement that you once felt. Alternatively, if you believe that your true feelings of love for someone have been revealed to you through a dream, then your unconscious may have been encouraging you to express your feelings for this person in the waking world.

Negative Interpretations: Did you dream that you were madly in love with someone who did not reciprocate your affections? If this person is your real-life partner, then your dream may have been mirroring your feelings of insecurity with regard to the strength of your relationship. Otherwise, was the object of your dream self's love someone you are attracted to, but who you fear does not have similar feelings for you? Or were you troubled by a dream in which you were in love with someone whom you consider to be an inappropriate object of such affection? For example, you may have felt this way if you, or the person whom your dream self was in love with, are already in a settled relationship with someone else in the waking world. If so, your unconscious may have been trying to force you to acknowledge your real-life feelings of attraction, or even genuine love for, this person, as disturbing as this may be to your conscious mind. Remember, the dream world is a safe environment in which to explore and help resolve your feelings, because, no matter what happens, no harm is actually done to anyone in the real world.

The Emotional Rollercoaster

Lust

The sexual urge is so strongly inherent in human nature, it is no wonder that it often makes its way into our dreams. And because sexual desire is such a basic and powerful drive, and yet there are so many social strictures surrounding sex, most people are likely to react to their erotic dreams with extreme emotions, either positive or negative.

Symbolic and Verbal Associations
› Sexual desire; ecstasy
› Urges or desires perceived as being "obscene" or "dirty"
› Repression; guilt

Positive Interpretations: Did you have a dream in which you sexually desired someone whom you also lust after in the real world? If so, then your dream was probably just mirroring your waking attraction to him or her. But if you dreamed that you felt desire for a stranger of the opposite sex, then you may have encountered your anima (the feminine aspects of your character, if you are a man) or your animus (the masculine aspects of your character, if you are a woman), possibly symbolizing your unconscious longing to unite or better integrate your masculine and feminine qualities. Also, since sex can be an act that leads to procreation, your dream self's sexual desire may have been an unconscious reference to the stirring of your creative powers. And if your dream depicted you actually having sex with someone to whom you are strongly attracted in the waking world, then your dream was probably a form of wish-fulfillment—though if you have been feeling unattractive or unlovable during your waking hours, your unconscious may also have been attempting to boost your self-esteem.

Negative Interpretations: Though erotic dreams are quite normal, if you are feeling sexually unfulfilled in the real world, then your sex drive may be compelled to seek its release in dreamland. And if you think sexual frustration may be the reason for your erotic dreams, the implications may not be entirely negative, as these dreams may offer you enlightenment or insight into your sexual desires. The same can be said if you had an erotic dream that disturbed or upset you, as it is important to remember that dream-land is a safe space in which the unconscious may experiment with your sexual urges. So if you are a heterosexual who dreamed that you lusted after someone of the same sex, your unconscious may have been exploring your feelings of, or else your curiosity about, same-sex sexual attraction; however, it is also possible that your dream was simply emphasizing the intensely intimate emotional relationship that you enjoy with this person. Many sexual dreams have a nonsexual meaning. For example, if you are a woman who feels guilty because you dreamed that you lusted after your brother-in-law (whom you like but you would never consider sleeping with), it may be that you would like to have a closer, more intimate (but nonsexual) relationship with him.

Relief

When we suffer physically or emotionally, the sudden absence of suffering may seem like the sweetest, most pleasurable sensation possible. Sometimes the unconscious may provide us with a temporary relief from our suffering in the form of a compensatory or wish-fulfillment dream in which we are released from whatever pain we have been enduring.

Symbolic and Verbal Associations

› Release; liberation
› Respite or reprieve; relief from pain or mental anguish
› Taking a break or a rest
› Receiving help or assistance

Positive Interpretations: Did a dream cause a feeling of relief to wash over you? If so, what did your dream self feel relieved from? If you are in some legal trouble in the real world, for instance, and you dreamed that it was all just a big mistake, then you most likely experienced a wish-fulfilling, escapist fantasy that your unconscious concocted in order to provide you with some temporary peace of mind. Likewise, if you suffer from chronic pain during your waking hours and you had a dream in which the pain was miraculously taken away, your unconscious was probably attempting both to fulfill your sincere wish for your misery to end and to give you a temporary respite from your suffering. If there is a daunting load of work before you in the waking world, did you have a dream in which someone came and offered to help you? In this case, your unconscious may have been signifying that this person is able to offer you some sort of assistance in the real world (though not necessarily in the way that was depicted in your dream). For example, if you are remodeling your home and you have been saving money by doing much of the labor yourself—a task that has proven much harder than you ever thought it would be—did you dream that your uncle, a retired carpenter, came to help you? If so, your uncle may not be willing or able to help you to actually do the work on your house, but he may be able to give you some good advice that will make your job a lot easier! In all of these examples, the purpose of your unconscious may also have been to hearten and encourage you in your time of trouble.

Negative Interpretations: If you had a dream in which you were relieved from some pain or suffering that you have been experiencing in the real world, you may have felt somewhat disappointed and saddened upon waking and realizing that it was only a dream. If this is the case, you should ask yourself what is causing you to suffer, and if there is anything that you can do to change your situation in the real world. For instance, if you are suffering from drug or alcohol addiction, and you dreamed that you had beaten your addiction and were living "clean," your unconscious may have been encouraging you to seek help in freeing yourself from your addiction in the waking world.

Sadness

Though they may leave us weeping, dreams of being sad are not always completely negative. On the contrary, these dreams may serve some very important functions, such as informing us about the nature or cause of our waking unhappiness, bringing repressed feelings out into the open, and providing an outlet for buried emotional pain.

Symbolic and Verbal Associations

> Grief
> Melancholy
> Depression
> Loss
> Emotional release; catharsis

Positive Interpretations: Did you have a dream in which you were so overcome with sadness that when you woke up you were weeping uncontrollably? If so, it is probable that there is some cause for sadness or grief in your waking life, though you may have repressed your feelings rather than allowing yourself to face them head on. Since emotional release is important to mental health, your unconscious may have been providing a cathartic outlet for your sadness via your dreams; this may be especially true if you are a person who rarely, if ever, allows yourself to cry during your waking hours. And, though you may have woken from your dream with a feeling of melancholy, you probably also felt somewhat relieved.

Negative Interpretations: Sometimes our dreams may enlighten as to the underlying reason or reasons for our feelings of sadness or depression, especially when we have pushed these painful feelings out of our waking consciousness. Can you remember what caused your dream self to feel sad? Dreams of grieving for someone who has actually died can usually be taken at face value. However, there may be a number of explanations for a dream in which you grieved for someone who is still alive. For instance, your unconscious may have chosen this person to represent something in your life that you feel you have lost, or else something that you'd like to rid yourself of, or it may be that you fear that your relationship with this person is in jeopardy; however, if the person you dreamed of is actually ill, or if you feel they are in some sort of danger, your dream may have been your unconscious's way of trying to prepare you for the worst. If you dreamed that you were saddened by having failed to achieve a goal or having missed an important opportunity, your dream may also have been fairly literal. Whatever the specifics of your dream sadness, you will probably find it helpful to try to think through its meaning rationally, during your waking hours. Finally, if you often find yourself grief-stricken or crying in your dreams, your unconscious may be highlighting a general depression, in which case you should consider seeking professional help.

Part 3:

Monitoring
Your Dreams

Recording Your Dreams

'You see things; and you say, "Why?" But I dream things that never were; and I say, "Why not?"'

George Bernard Shaw

Even when you've developed your skills in interpreting your dreams, you'll gain far more from your unconscious mind's nocturnal messages if you record them. Why? Well, very few people have faultless memories, and it's entirely possible that you will forget a potentially significant dream sooner or later. Having a written record of it will preserve it so that it doesn't disappear for good. Another reason for writing up your dreams is that having an archive of dream material – essentially, raw data – to analyse may help you identify any dream themes, trends, and patterns. Maybe, by comparing your dream diary with your everyday diary, you will be able to link them with real-world triggers.

The following pages contain advice on ways of capturing your dreams on paper before they fade from your memory. You'll also find hints on ways of interpreting them.

Write down whatever you can remember that may have significance in your dream recordings. It's advisable to note at the very least the date, or dates, on which you had the relevant dream, or dreams, as well as to read the relevant sections of the symbolism in Part 2, to try to work out what your dream could have meant, and to make a note of this, too.

Interpreting Dreams

Keeping a Dream Diary

It is crucial that you scribble down, or dictate, the details of a dream as soon as you wake up; leave it any longer, and you run the risk that they'll elude your powers of recollection.

Later on, you may find it helpful to write up your dream in full from your initial notes according to a set format, such as the example given below. You could copy down this format in your diary or create a similar template on your computer to fill in yourself. As your dream diary grows, you could keep its pages or documents in a dedicated binder, card index, or computer folder.

Indexing Your Dreams

Remember to create an index to your dreams, and to update it every time you add a new dream, to make locating and referring to a particular dream, and perhaps also categorizing your dreams, easier.

Dream Diary: Example Format

Dream number[1]:
Dreamtype(s)[2]:
Day of the week:
Date:
Title:
The prevalent atmosphere/how you were feeling:
The setting:
The characters:
What happened?
Any puns or punning imagery?
Possible trigger:
Possible interpretation:
Possible message:
Possible link with dream number:

Explanatory Notes

1. Number your dreams in the order in which you have them. When it comes to analysing your dreams, you'll find identifying and referring to dream "5" a lot more convenient than to "the nightmare about my computer."

2. For example: literal, factual, processing, physiological; punning; problem-solving; inspirational; cathartic or safety-valve; contrary, compensatory, wish fulfilment; recurring; nightmare; anxiety; precognitive; telepathic.

Dream Diary: Sample Entry

Dream number: 5
Dream type(s): literal; nightmare; precognitive (?)
Day of the week: Thursday
Date: (include day, month, and year)
Title: Computer Catastrophe!
The prevalent atmosphere/how you were feeling:
   initially relaxed, even complacent; then fraught;
   eventually panicked and despairing
The setting: my office
The characters: me; my great-aunt Prudence; my pet
   mouse Clutterbuck
What happened? I was typing the final words of
   a novel, which I somehow knew had taken me
   years to write and rewrite until I believed it was
   the best I could make it, when I clicked "Save." I
   was concerned when the computer didn't seem to
   respond, and then became increasingly panic-
   stricken when the screen turned black and clicking
   the mouse and hitting the keys didn't have any
   effect. The computer had died, and I'd lost my
   bestseller! I was distraught! Then Aunt Prudence
   appeared by my side, clutching Clutterbuck, my
   pet mouse, and said, "Better safe than sorry!".
   Then I woke up.
Any puns or punning imagery? Clutterbuck could
   have represented my computer mouse.
Possible trigger: Spending the previous day inputting
   important information into my computer.

Possible interpretation: I am unconsciously aware that I am risking losing my work by not copying it and storing it safely, or by keeping it only in a cloud space that could be hacked. My dream was urging me to mend my careless ways by exposing me to this worst-case scenario, and reinforced the message by conjuring up Aunt Prudence to impart her words of wisdom.

Possible message: Back up everything on my computer that I would be devastated to lose.

Possible link with dream number: 2

Indexed Summary

Dream Number: 5
Date: May 19, 20**
Title: Computer Catastrophe
Type: literal; nightmare; precognitive (?)

Selected Further Reading

The Interpretation of Dreams, by Sigmund Freud, first published in German as *Die Traumdeutung* in 1900, and in English in 1913; available in several modern editions. A radical text that proposed a direct connection between our dreams and the ideas in our unconscious mind, or "id"—ideas suppressed by the "ego" during our waking hours. Dreams, according to Freud, are wish-fulfilment fantasies that we can learn to interpret.

Modern Man in Search of a Soul, by Carl Jung, 1933. A collection of essays derived from Jung's lectures, the book includes an essay on dream analysis that shows how his ideas on the function and interpretation of dreams had developed and diverged from Freud's. Jung believed that dreams "give information about the secrets of the inner life and reveal to the dreamer hidden factors of his personality."

Dreaming: A Conceptual Framework for Philosophy of Mind and Empirical Research, by Jennifer M. Windt, 2015. Bringing together the neuroscience of dreaming and the philosophy of mind, this is a comprehensive and detailed study of how the body and external stimuli influence the contents of our dreams, and what is happening when we dream.

When Brains Dream: Exploring the Science and Mystery of Sleep, by Antonio Zadra and Robert Stickgold, 2021. A wide-ranging study of dream research by two academics that provides a comprehensive history of theories of dream physiology, content and function, as well as presenting new ideas and theories of their own.

The Author

Clare Gibson is a writer and historian specialising in art history and how to interpret symbols. Her previous works include *The Secret Life of Dreams* (Sterling), *How to Read Symbols* (A&C Black), and *The Hidden Life of Ancient Egypt, The Hidden Life of Art, The Hidden Life of Renaissance Art*, and *Symbols of the Goddess*, published by Saraband.